ART, IDEOLOGY AND SOCIAL COMMITMENT IN AFRICAN POETRY

ART, IDEOLOGY AND SOCIAL COMMITMENT IN AFRICAN POETRY

Udenta O. Udenta

KRAFT BOOKS LIMITED

Published by
Kraft Books Limited
6A Polytechnic Road, Sango, Ibadan
Box 22084, University of Ibadan Post Office
Ibadan, Oyo State, Nigeria
℘ + 234 (0)803 348 2474, + 234 (0)805 129 1191
E-mail: kraftbooks@yahoo.com
www.kraftbookslimited.com

© Udenta O. Udenta, 2015

First published 2015

ISBN 978-978-918-224-4 (Paperback)
ISBN 978-978-918-285-5 (Hardback)

First published in 1993 by
Fourth Dimension Publishing Co. Ltd.
16th Fifth Avenue, City Layout, P.M.B. 01164
Enugu, Nigeria

All Rights Reserved

First printing, March 2015

Dedication

To the little ones, but now not so little;
Queenette Chinenye, Ndubuisi, Chibuzo and Acho:
May your generation find joy, happiness and
fulfilment on the promise of our present-day labour
And
To your dad and mum,
Sam and Fidel,
For giving you life and succour

Acknowledgements

In an environment where gross materialism has been institutionalized as a way of life, it is obviously very difficult to find people who are still motivated by sublime desires and noble thoughts. The problem becomes compounded when such an environment's moral foundation has collapsed, leaving in its wake the ashes of spiritual sterility and ethical idiocy. I salute Dr. Arthur Nwankwo, a rare gem among his generation, whose incurable optimism about the power of intellect and moral authority as the only way forward for our people has really ennobled me. He is truly an inspirer.

I salute the following members of my generation who believe that we have the potential to harness our inherent possibilities despite the present reign of unbelief: Barrister Patrick Ugochukwu, Chief Ogbonna Onuoha, Mr. Okechukwu Okeke, Mr. Uzoma Nwokocha, Dr. Aja Akpuru Aga, Mr. Bob Ogu, Dr. Ikonne, and the late Mr. Udo Nwokocha. As my colleagues at Abia State University, Uturu I have indeed learnt a lot from you.

My colleagues at the Centre for Igbo Studies deserve a worthy mention here for without their encouragement, support and understanding, the completion of this research would have suffered a serious setback. I mention in this regard Dr. U. D. Anyanwu, Rev. Fr. Dr. Jude U. Aguwa, Mr. Emmanuel Inyama and Mr. Okechukwu Okoro.

Finally, I salute the patience and thoroughness with which the staff of the "Office" went through this work and organized for its publication. Remain blessed.

Preface

In the preface to my *Revolutionary Aesthetics and the African Literary Process,* I made a promise that I will redress the imbalance in that study by writing and publishing a book devoted to African Poetry. Actually, I had virtually completed a research work on this subject when the book was published but I felt that something still needs to be said about African fiction and drama. Hence the publication of my *Ideological Sanction and Social Action in African Literature* (now re-issued as *Heroism and Critical Consciousness in African Poetry*), which together with the present volume, is hoped to constitute an integral study of modern African literature, at least from my chosen ideo-aesthetic perspective. I said as much in the preface to the work on Ideological Sanction.

My first joy is thus predicated on the fact that my assigned task has been performed. There is yet a critical perspective on selected theoretical and textual issues in modern African literature which will hopefully join the three previous studies before long, as a further clarification of the burning research issues that have captured my attention since the mid-1980s. Modern African poetry, just as its fiction and drama counterparts, is a product of two distinct socio-aesthetic forces: the received traditionalist aesthetic practices and the aesthetics overdetermined by the complex forces incarnated by colonialism. When the creative individuality of the different creative artists is added to the two, the picture is one of a complex, highly diverse and stimulating artistic tradition. The explication of what this poetic tradition means to us, and in that connection an investigation into its social relevance must, of necessity, take these issues into consideration.

Nevertheless, it is my belief that this picture is not a complete one. When a researcher adopts a stated ideological and aesthetic position in the examination of national and continental literature, certain comparative considerations become fore-grounded, that, one, may be a product of that frame and terms of reference, and, two, may lead to the desideratum of other issues not accommodated by conventional techniques of analyzing acclaimed generic materials.

This is exactly the case with modern African poetry, especially when the research into its ontological status and identity requires the deployment of ideological and aesthetic categories consistent with the researcher's set objectives. My investigation into modern African poetry, from the revolutionary aesthetic stand point confronts the colonial and colonial aesthetic norms which the prevalent critical orthodoxy had for long assumed to have conditioned its emergence. That exercise has been both an eye-opener, and a rewarding venture.

If the present study succeeds in opening a new vista of knowledge about modern African poetry that helps in re-directing attention to previously concealed forces that shape that vibrant tradition, especially in our de-mythicizing milieu pertaining, but not limited, to even my chosen ideo-aesthetic method, I would feel re-assured that my set objective has been accomplished.

O.U. Udenta
September, 1996

Preface to the Second Edition

This second edition is coming out 18 years after the book was originally published in 1996. A lot have occurred in-between, both in my personal life and the shifts and transformations it took in a two decade period, and in the deeper understanding, by African cultural and literary producers and the scholars and critics who mediate their productions, of the ontology of African literature and the aesthetic and ideological formations it undergirds. I completed the original draft of the work in 1986 –1987, the same time as I completed the drafts of *Revolutionary Aesthetics and the African Literary Process, Ideological Sanction and Social Action in African Literature* (re-issued now as *Heroism and Critical Consciousness in African Literature*) and *Art, Society and Identity: Essays On African Literature* (published for the first time in 2014 after a 22-year wait!)

While these works are different in the genres they treated, I have taken the advantage of their 'second coming', as it were, to illuminate their interesting history over the intervening period, because it took an incredible time for this second edition to see the light of day and their reception by students, researchers and scholars since their original publication. I did all that in a very lengthy 'Preface' to the second edition of *Revolutionary Aesthetics and the African Literary Process*. And because that work and *Art, Ideology and Social Commitment in African Poetry* received the widest critical attention and scrutiny, the 'Preface' under reference has much to say about the two books. It will not be worth the effort repeating here the views and arguments I canvassed elsewhere, and while it is not my intention to compel potential readers to buy a book they have little use for, my advice is that an encounter with what I consider a well made argument in that 'Preface' will be absolutely necessary for a deeper interrogation and understanding of some of the broad ontological, aesthetic and ideological issues germane to the construction of the current work.

I have taken the advantage of this revised edition to not only rework great portions of it, correct the noted grammatical and linguistic deficiencies of the original effort but most crucially to bring the discourse up to speed with the aesthetic currents of the past one and half decades. While the first edition dealt with African poetic craft up to the late 1980s and early 1990s, this second edition has tried to push the debate well into the 21st century. To realize this vision of a more contemporary critical engagement with African poetic experience, I added two new chapters to the work. The first, titled "The Aesthetic and Cultural Context of Post-2000 Nigerian Poetry", limits the discourse to a national literature – that of Nigeria – on the hope and the expectation that artistic, aesthetic, cultural and ideological categories therein could be abstracted for a continent-wide application. The second additional chapter captioned "South African Poetry After 1994 and the Postcolonial Debate" pushes the discourse from Part Five of the first edition titled "Poetry and Politics in Apartheid South Africa" to accommodate the post-apartheid poetic consciousness in South Africa that is substantially defined by the robust ontological debates around postcolonial cultural and identity formation, postmodern sensibility and revolutionary aesthetic imperatives in South African poetry.

Structurally, I have retained the spirit of the original composition while noting the comments by a number of critics about its simple, linear, progressive historical mode. It would not have been extremely difficult to reconstruct the entire project around structural categories determined by ideo-aesthetic imperatives and re-insert on the poetic sites epistemic forces that may transgress or even outrightly subvert the notion of historical linearity. However, in the course of my fairly extensive research in preparation of the second edition of my works, I became deeply immersed in Fredric Jameson's construct on history, literature and ideology, and more specifically his conception of dialectical criticism and categoric synthesis that encompasses reflexive thinking, utopian thinking, historicizing thinking and totalizing thinking. The dangers of such a deconstructive mode of reasoning, investigation and presentation, if I had carried it out, even in the context of an ontological assumption that is situated on revolutionary aesthetic possibility, is that it could lead not only to emptied out stylizations that are devoid of historicity but may consequent in the breakdown of the signifying chain of reality-apprehension. Thus, my less than adequate intellectual preparation of the first draft has been legitimated by my more profound understanding of the benefit of periodizing hypothesis, historical periodization and periodization in dominance theoretic construct in realizing my initial objective intention.

Finally, it is important to stress, as I did elsewhere with regard to *Revolutionary Aesthetics and the African Literary Process,* that after all is said and done the present effort is little more than an apprentice craft composed by a 22 year-old student who was just about to earn his Masters degree when the initial draft was completed. Its modest strengths and very glaring weaknesses are products of a youthful energy. Yet I believe that it has important messages it communicated about African poetry; messages that still resonate with a trenchant force in African postcolonial spaces under increasing pressure from the spatializing pyrotechnics of late, postmodern capitalism and a victim of the new form of historical depthlessness, cultural ambiguities and de-territorialized and hybridized identity it currently and persistently excretes.

Udenta O. Udenta
Abuja November, 2014

Author's Note

I wrote the conclusion to this book about 1987 and have virtually retained it, unchanged even in the context of this new edition of the work. My insights on the spatialization of African cultural spaces by post-modernism and post-structuralism; the metaphor of Lampedusa which more than describes the one-way traffic by African cultural and intellectual elite from the African postcolonial margins to the polis; and the social liminality of the Diaspora into which have been inserted the forces of hybridization, deterritorialization, normativized translocational values and alteritirized, contingent, ambivalent and temporarized human identity – even at the nascent stages of the canonization of the post-modern and post-structuralist variant of postcolonial theory by Edward Said, Homi Bhabha and Gayatri Spivak – is profoundly striking.

Content

Dedication 5
Acknowledgements 6
Preface 7
Preface to the Second Edition 9
Author's Note 12

Introduction 15

Part One
Revolutionary Poetry: A Socio-historical Overview 19

Part Two
Genesis of Art and Ideology in African Poetry:
Negritude and Nationalist Poetry 37
i. Negritude Poetry: Francophone Africa 39
ii. 'Nationalist' Poetry: Anglophone Africa 51

Part Three
Art and Ideology in Postcolonial African Poetry:
The Critical Realist/Radical Liberal
Humanist Context 65

Part Four
Art and Ideology in the Period of Re-colonization
The Revolutionary Aesthetic Imperative 106

Part Five
The Aesthetic and Cultural Contexts of Post-2000
Nigerian Poetry... 139

Part Six
Poetry and Politics in Apartheid South Africa............ 174

Part Seven
South African Poetry after 1994 and the
Postcolonial Debate... 185

Conclusion.. 217

Bibliography.. 220

Index... 224

INTRODUCTION

One way of introducing our subject is to pose the all necessary question: What do modern African poets write about? Modern African poetry is an interventionist genre, an art form which, having assimilated the rich resources of African social experience, mediates them in a creative mode. Modern African poets, as purveyors of this socio-aesthetic consciousness, thus write about those things which are meaningful to the African, both as a private individual and as a member of a social community[1]: his passions and his desires, his great aspirations and social affirmations, the character and structure of the polity, freedom, justice and social change.

In examining the social responsibility of modern African poetry, it is fashionable for conventional scholarship[2] to establish a dichotomy between the social commitment of traditional poetic modes of communication and the adjudged privatist ruminations of modern poetic creations. The missing link in this scheme has remained the separation of

---

[1] This expression is an adumbration of Georg Lukacs' view in Studies in European Realism (London: Monlin Press, 1950), in which he sees great realism as embracing a three-dimensionality: Man the artist as a mediating agent, man as private individual, and as a member of a human community.

[2] "Conventional Scholarship" describes the research activities of Eurocentric critics who evaluate African literature, and art in general, from perspectives and with criteria consistent with Western notions of aesthetics. It is essentially the summary-commentary style of analysis which locates themes, structure, artistic forms

the formal, contentual and contextual properties of art; that is, to examine art from mutually exclusive perspectives. While it is obvious that the form of traditional poetry is substantially determined by the mode of verbal delivery which makes for immediacy, spontaneity and evaluative and interpretative audience response, as against the private craft of the individual modern poet who work via text, the essential fact still remains that both traditions are socially relevant to the burning issues of the day.[3]

It is therefore pertinently clear that African poetry has been playing a vital role in society since its emergence. What, of course, must be stressed is that the social commitment of African poetry is conditioned, in the main, by the character of the historical age, the relationship between the practitioners of art and the ruling establishment, and the exclusive or inclusive nature of the social formation. Traditional poetry was an affirmative art, with minor exceptions here and there, because it was an art whose aspirations were essentially conterminous with the logic of the social order. As chanters, griots, recounters and repositors of cultural, spiritual and even mystical values, the traditional poet was an integral member of his society whose knowledge and wisdom were respected, valued and adhered to.

Colonialism was a disruptive social phenomenon. It excluded, rather than included social elements whose perception of reality was diametrically opposed to its worldview. The end result was the use of the protest tradition in literature, politics and culture, by an elite most of who desired, not an inclusion in the colonial structure of power,

---

[3] Even in the poems of Wole Soyinka and the early Okigbo which have been adjudged obscure, privatist and socially irrelevant (see for example, Chinweizu, et al, Toward the Decolonization of African Literature, Enugu: Fourth Dimension 1980), a proper socio-aesthetic investigation discovers abiding social commitment beneath the veneer of imposed obscurantist linguistic and stylistic forms.

but a re-interpretation and redefinition of power on the basis of freedom and national sovereignty.

There was actually a thin dividing line between African social experience and the artistic response to it in colonial and postcolonial discourses. The protest tradition was carried over to the latter because the emergent black leadership in Africa, rather than re-interpret and re-define their understanding of power in favour of the urgency of the radical re-humanization of their people and the retrieval of their societies' cultural integrity, became more enthusiastic than the erstwhile colonial forces in cementing social inequality, political oppression, the mismanagement of national resources and institutionalized corruption.

These tendencies are still noticeable in most African countries today, meaning for us that the protest tradition in modern African poetry is still dominant as a social- aesthetic category. The affirmative consciousness in modern African poetry will, thus, wait for the time and age when African societies are once more back on the road of all-inclusive reconstruction, to the extent that no dichotomy will exist between what the poets write about and the national development strategies of the managers of the state apparatus.

It will be quite clear to any reader of this work that I adopted the revolutionary aesthetic method in my research, just as I did in *Revolutionary Aesthetic and the African Literary Process* and *Ideological Sanction and Social Action in African Literature*. This method affords me the necessary perspicacity of vision and ability to domesticate a universal critical criterion to suit the temper and subjectivities of the African literary process. This process of domestication has inexorably led me to a re-definition and revaluation of that criterion in response to the wide-ranging transformational historical and cultural processes that characterize the African postcolonial moment.

The study is structured as a discourse; that is, the attempt is to examine all the issues in a continuous discursive mode that takes into account the historical periodization in the evolution of African nation states. The necessity of this approach stems from the inter-relationships and interconnections between the ontological, aesthetic and ideological forces worked into African poetic consciousness and sensibility to the extent that a mechanistic schematic separation will be patently artificial.

The study is divided into five parts. Part one deals with the historical formation and evolution of revolutionary poetry as a universal aesthetic phenomenon. Part two addresses the historical, aesthetic and ideological context and imperatives of African poetic productions during the colonial moment. Part three examines the critical ideo-aesthetic episteme that undergirds African poetic craft in the immediate postcolonial period. Part four focuses attention on the African poetic imagination in the contemporary postcolonial epoch. Part five is a critical comment on South African poetry during the apartheid era.

My research into modern African poetry has convinced me that no issue is quite as significant and socially relevant than the issue of art, ideology and social commitment. What I attempt doing here is to foreground, as a means of stimulating further research, the dimensions of these issues as they pertain to the ontological self-awareness and social relevance of a very vibrant African literary form.

Part One

REVOLUTIONARY POETRY: A SOCIO-HISTORICAL OVERVIEW

> Works of literature and art, as ideological forms, are products of the reflection in the human brain of the life of a given society. Revolutionary literature and art are the products of the reflection of the life of the people in the brains of revolutionary writers and artists. The life of the people is always a mine of the raw materials for literature and art, materials in their natural form, materials that are crude but most vital, rich and fundamental; they make all literature and art seem pallid by comparison; they provide literature and art with an inexhaustible source, their only source.[1] (Mao Tse-Tung)

Mao Tse-Tung's observation about revolutionary literature and art in general in the famous Henan Talks is particularly relevant to any study of revolutionary poetry, and the place of society in generating, sustaining and directing revolutionary poetic consciousness and sensibility. Truly, literature is a reflection of society in its moment of development and transformation, and poetry, much more than any other genre of literature, captures this mutative nature of objective reality intensely, poignantly and subtly.

Right from the dawn of human civilization, creative writers have been using the raw material of life as their point of departure in the apprehension of aesthetic consciousness. It is the degree of fidelity of the subjectively remolded aesthetic experience to the objective facts of existence, the degree of imaginativeness of the recreated reality, and the organic blend of idea-content and form that determine the success or otherwise of the artistic work.

It is to be understood that literature, despite reflecting objective reality in a concretely existing social formation, and in spite of being an ideological form, does not apprehend that reality in a direct, mechanical form of one-to-one naturalistic, photographic or illustrationistic correspondence.[2] Literature has its moments of greatness and moments of degeneration in all historical epochs and shows an unevenness of maturity that may not correspond to the process of development at the materialist phase of social progression. Apart from all the tendencies which specify literature's particular position as an ideological formation,[3] literature and art still show an upward development and progress that take cognizance of man's historical evolution from primitive communalism to the present period of contradictions between a rampant late, postmodern capitalism incarnated at the polis and the cultural, political and ideological resistance to it at several global geo-political and geo-strategic domains. Literature is therefore responsive to the laws of materialist dialectics and is dependent, in the long run, on the very social formation or socio-economic system that engenders it.

There is no doubt that Renaissance literary productions were qualitatively higher than the productions of the medieval times. There is also no doubt that the later Renaissance period – the age of enlightenment produced better, more advanced literary works than the early Renaissance period. There is little argument too, that the Romanticism and Idealism of late 18th century and early 19th century were advancements over Renaissance literature with its schematism, restricted rationalism, formalism and limited class outlook. 19th century realism – a product of emergent capitalism and the contradictions it generated – was in its harsh attack on individualism and philistinism, a far more developed literary form than 18th century Romanticism, not only in its mass quality, popularization of art and accessibility, but also in its emergence out of a qualitatively higher social formation. The same would be said of the art of the then socialist community in relation to bourgeois art either nascent or during the present late, postmodern and post-imperial epoch.

Revolutionary poetry, which is an important aspect of revolutionary literature, is not a 20th century phenomenon. It has been in existence since the slave social formation and other subsequent epochs in human history. The part revolutionary ideas played in its development is to give it the right ideological touch, the right political tone, the correct consciousness and class partisanship, and to ground it firmly into the soil of dialectics. Slave songs, both in the plantations and in the mountains and other hideouts the slaves dwell to fight the slave owners, were concrete poetic expressions of their revolutionary zeal and enthusiasm. In the medieval ages, feudal serfs and peasants composed poems and songs which affirmed their humanity and their right to existence. One such poem in Medieval France declared that "when Adam delved and Eve spawned nobody was then a gentleman" to the taunts by the Feudal lords and the landed aristocracy that the peasants were "Misshapen as Monsters."[4]

But revolutionary poetry was given a fundamental boost in the 19th century because of the emergence of industrial capitalism and the development of large urban mega polis; the harsh conditions of working in the factories and living in the shanties; the increasing maturity of the political consciousness of the proletariat occasioned by the rise of revolutionary ideas – founded by Marx and Engels; and the combination of both the tactics and strategies of intellectual and ideological class struggle with the tactics and strategies of armed political struggle. The socio-political and socio-economic climate in Europe moreover favoured the emergence of a radical tradition in literature, and especially poetry, as most of the European nations were engaged in one form of nationalist war of ethnic and cultural identity or the other, and at the same time were contending with the challenges posed by the working class movement.

One of such poetic creations of this period was the song of the Silesian weavers, more popularly called the Weavers' Song which influenced Karl Marx greatly in its historically correct ideological vision and consciousness of the place of the proletariat in the overall context of the revolutionary struggle. In the words of S.S. Prawer:

> One literary production of 1844 appeared to Marx of special significance. This was a poem written during the revolt of the Silesian weavers in that year and sung by those weavers in their marches. (From the poem, he saw the revolutionary will of the 'proletarian Cinderella' to whom he prophesied an "athletic stature" in the not too distant future.) The weavers' song... thus occupies an important place in Marx's literary gallery. It signifies in his eyes, the transition from old folk-song to new proletarian poetry.[5] (Emphasis mine)

Marx's own personal assessment of the historical significance of the Weavers' Song is important here in order to place on record his own objective appraisal of that phenomenon, and not just an adumbration of his position as we have already done. Marx asserts:

> Not a single one of the French and English workers' revolts possessed so theoretical and conscious a character as the revolt of the Silesian weavers. Remember, first of all, the Weavers song, that bold call to battle in which domestic hearth, factory, district are not so much as mentioned; in which, rather, the proletariat shouts its opposition to a

society based on private property in a striking, trenchant, ruthless, and violent way. The Silesian revolt begins with the very thing with which the French and English workers' revolt ends: with conscious understanding of what the proletariat is.[6]

Before the emergence of the Silesian weavers' song, another workers' revolt in Lyons, France, had already led to the creation of an important revolutionary poem. This was in 1831, thirteen years before the Silesian revolt and the composition of the Weavers' Song. The song titled 'Song of the Silk-Weavers of Lyons' (chant des canuts) is described by S.S. Prawer as showing at least as much "conscious understanding of what the proletariat is".[7] Heine, one of the revolutionary poets of this period, significantly enough, used this song as a model of his poem on the deprivation and tenacity of the Silesian weavers. The projection of this revolutionary poetry was made possible through the instrumentality of the few existing radical journals that could tolerate such a tendency. Revolutionary intellectuals and political activists like Marx, Engels and Heine were some of the contributors to such journal as *Forwards!* where such poems and other revolutionary writings were published. In Prawer's words:

> Both Marx's commentary on 'Bloody ASSIZE' and Heine's poem "The poor Weavers" (later renamed "The Silesian Weavers") appeared in a radical German journal started in Paris at the beginning of 1844. It was entitled Forwards! (Vorwaits!). Its executive editor was Heinrich Bornstein, and its contributors included Marx, Engels, Heine, Herwegh, Georg Weerth and Bakunin.[8]

An organic relationship, therefore, exists between workers' revolutionary poetry and protest and the intellectual, political and ideological defenders and champions of the cause of proletarian liberation in the mid-19th century period.

It was not only the workers who created revolutionary

poetry out of the living conditions of their struggle; the radical intelligentsia also demonstrated their class solidarity by writing revolutionary poetry of the first order. Karl Marx himself tried his hand in poetry, a subject he so dearly loved, and only failed to reach the height of greatness in that direction because of the more pressing tasks of creating a scientific basis of the workers political struggle and building a formidable organizational structure on which that struggle could draw strength.[9] Apart from Marx, people like George Weerth and George Harwegh, devoted so much time in the 19th century to the composition of poems illustrating the historic mission and task of the working class, their endurance and determination in the face of oppression, and their firm belief in the inevitable triumph of a new revolutionary order. Drawing image-imperatives from the raw materials of existing objective reality and metaphors from the living struggle itself – both theoretical and practical – they conveyed the sense of urgency of the struggle and rallied their readers and listeners to the call of liberation and freedom. As D. Markov argues:

> The writings of Georg Harwegh, Ferdinand Freiligrath and George Weerth constitute another illustrious chapter in the history of world revolutionary literature. Their poetry, filled with a sense of social commitment, rallied its readers to the contribution of this literature. An example was the poetry of Weerth.[10]

It is important to add here that F. Engels referred to Weerth "as the first and most significant poet of the German proletariat".[11] These German poets were not the only revolutionary poets of the period. In France, which has consistently led other European nations in revolutionary uprisings (1789, 1848 and 1872), revolutionary tradition in poetry had already taken root, culminating in the epochal Paris Commune where workers for the first time in history seized power from their oppressors and held it for a long while. The poetry that emerged out of that experience; in short, the poetry of the Paris Commune was a giant stride in the development of revolutionary poetry. Eugene Pottier, Jules Valles and others contributed immensely to that tradition. As a critic noted:

> Revolutionary ideas were also introduced to literature by poets of the Paris Commune, Eugene Pottier, Jean Clement, Jules Valles. There is a clear link to be observed between their work and the revolutionary literature of other countries. "The Internationale" composed by Eugene Potter represented the poetic expression of the revolutionary solidarity of the working people and soon was to become the international anthem of the proletariat.[12]

Lenin himself said of Pottier that he was "one of the greatest propagandists by song".[13]

This cursory look at the broad lines of development of revolutionary poetry in Western Europe in the 19th century illustrates, though incompletely, the main tendencies of that phenomenon. We detect a maturing poetic sensibility with the correspondent maturing of poetic vision; the increasing participation of the workers in the process of creating revolutionary poetry; and the unity of the ideological struggle with the more decisive political and armed struggle.

Similar tendencies were particularly noticeable in other regions of the world, especially in Latin America and the Caribbean where revolutionary poetry played an active part in the dismantling of colonial imperialism and the establishment of many independent governments. The acute class contradictions engendered by the repressive colonial socio-economic formation, the deepening of the crisis of imperialism itself, the open barbarization of the people and their precarious material existence, all acted as imperatives that sustained the revolutionary ethos in society, poetry included. The poets of that period became increasingly class conscious, politically and ideologically committed and used their works to advance the cause of national liberation. This direction of Caribbean poetry was also the direction of the revolutionary poetry of Eastern European countries, especially the countries of the Balkan. A comparative study of the poetry of these two regions will reveal homology of vision, similar political sentiments expressed in poetry, and the proletarian class loyalty of most of the poets of the period.

The Balkan region has been for centuries the theater for both feudal repressors, religious expansionists (Christian and Moslem) and callous empire-builders. Decapitated many times, reduced to tiny cleavages in more than one occasion, having changed hands between subsequent conquerors, and denied statehood for a considerable historical time, "Balkanization" – derived from the Balkans – has come to stay in our Lexicon as a synonym of fragmentation, decapitation, willful division and flexible boundaries. Nevertheless, centuries of repression and subjugation have been incapable of suppressing the rebellious spirit of the people and their desire for freedom and political independence. These centuries of struggles and agitations culminated in the development of a viable working class and progressive peasant movement in the 19th century. Responsive to and influenced by the working class movement in Western Europe, the workers and radical intellectuals and revolutionaries of Poland, Bulgaria, Czech, Slovakia and Russia began to lay both a firm foundation and a formidable tradition for the all round struggle of national emancipation, and in that attempt saw in poetry a great potential as a purveyor of revolutionary ideas. In Poland, for example:

> Revolutionary songs achieved wide spread popularity in early proletarian literature. Songs like Waclam Swiecicki's "Warsaw Song," Boleslaw Czervenski's "Red Banner" and Ludwik Warnynski's "Mazurka Chains" written in the 1880s became enormously popular in progressive circles of polish society. Similar popularity was also enjoyed by songs written somewhat later, such as "To the Barricades", or "Mary

March". These were quickly taken up by the workers and were to be heard at demonstrations and other mass gatherings.[14] (Emphasis mine.)

This shows incontrovertibly that the poets of this period were responsive to the revolutionary struggle of the workers and were identifying with it. It also demonstrates that the poet of the time "has merged with the working masses and is filled with admiration for their great potential".[15] Waclaw Swiecicki's "Warsaw song", a stanza of which runs thus:

> But we shall rally round the red banner, Staunchly and proudly to go into battle, Fight for the great cause of all working people, A better world, brotherhood, holy freedom,

And the following passage from a poem by Frantisek Josef Hlavacek from the then Czechoslovakia:

> The proletarian army, With its red banner, unfurled is inexorably marching Ranks serried, visage stem....

Are demonstrations of this close affinity and common bond between the revolutionary poet and the proletariat, between the ideological struggle and political struggle.

The spirit of revolutionary poetry was sustained in the period in both the Czech and Slovakia republics by Ladislav Zapotocky, Josef Bolesav Pecka (whose "Let the Song of Brotherhood Strike Fear into the Rich" was particularly popular and loved) and Norbert Zocela. In Bulgaria, it was Georgi Kirkov ("Workers' Songs" and "March of the Workers") in particular, that pioneered this tradition. The same tendency was noticeable in Russia where Leonard Radin ("Forward Bravely in Step"), Filip Shkulev ("We the Blacksmiths"), Alexander Bogdanov-Volzhsky ("Song of the Proletariat"), and Gleb Krzhizhanovsky ("Let Tyrants Rage") strengthened the revolutionary poetic spirit of the time and used their art to further the struggle. Most of these poems carried widespread popularity at the time, helped in galvanizing the workers to action and were heard in workers' rallies and gatherings.

Most of these poems embody aesthetic and emotional sensibilities and are "expressed through symbols, allegories, metaphors and rhetoric".[16] This could be seen in "Red", a poem by Kosta Abrasevic, Serbia's first proletarian poet, where the expression "Ruby-red" is associated with "blood" and "Mighty veins," "lighting and "dark sky" all showed the inevitable triumph of the workers and the crushing defeat of tyrants. The last three lines of the poem depict this clearly:

> Ruby-red anger sets fists tightly clenching: Tremble ye, tyrants, our vengeance is nigh Ruby-red. It will be bloody and dire.

Images of this nature also abound in the works of the revolutionary poets of this period, especially in the works of Dimitry Polyanov, the founder of proletarian poetry in Bugaria.

The 20th century was, much more than the 19th century, a time of turbulent changes and social upheavals. Capitalism, for one, had been transformed in the later part of the 19th century and the early part of the 20th century into an international imperialist system. Contradictions hitherto unknown in the past were brought to the fore because of the greed, insatiable appetite and avarice of imperialist nations and conglomerates to sap the material resources of the dependent and semi-dependent nations. V. I. Lenin, the century's greatest political philosopher and revolutionary strategist captured this forcefully in his book, *Imperialism, the Highest Stage of Capitalism*, where he exposed the tactics and methods of high finance capital to bring the world under a totalitarian, monopolistic cartel. The twentieth century was also an age when the working class movement achieved great significance as a force for social change. The political and social conditions of many nations favoured the emergence of viable working class organizations that were prepared to confront reactionary tendencies in all their diverse manifestations. The collapse of the Second International signalled the inevitable demise of social opportunism, ideological compromise and reactionary nationalism (manifestly taking the specific forms of Bernsteinism, Kautskyism and Economism) and their replacement by a consistent and clearly defined revolutionary ideological alternative.

In most of the developed capitalist countries, the proletariat was demanding for participation in the governance of the polity and in the restructuring of society along the path of justice and freedom. In the semi-dependent countries like Russia where local reaction had been acting as the hand-maiden of imperialism, the radical wing of the Russian Social Democratic Labour Party pioneered the movement for revolutionary changes. In other nations of Europe, especially in the Balkan countries, the working people were responding to the call for change and were decisively confronting their oppressors. Even in the colonies, the popular movement for national liberation was taking an increasing radical and genuinely anti-colonial, anti-imperialist and anti-racist line and was struggling for the dismantling of colonialism and imperialism.

The major hallmarks of the second decade of the century were the First Imperialist War of 1914-1918 when the contradictions of imperialism become so glaring and manifest that their resolution had to take the specific form of a major international conflagration, and the Russian Revolution of 1917. The latter phenomenon was so fundamental and significant because it was the first time that revolutionary ideas triumphed in any country which thus ushered in a new phase of human history: the phase of revolutionary transformation, not just as a political and ideological system, but as a concretely existing social system.

The significance of all these developments to literature, especially revolutionary poetry, is obvious because the literary artists of that time were observers, participants and commentators on the world situation, and, more importantly because literature, as a form of social consciousness, is organically interrelated with social being for its image imperatives and sources of signification. It is little surprise, therefore, that writers of democratic sympathies and progressive opinions crossed over to the side of the working class and used their art in concretizing the yearnings of the oppressed people in the literary sphere. By doing this, they were furthering the tradition of revolutionary and patriotic art started since the dawn of human history and which was given a decisive impetus in the 19th century.

In Czech and Slovakia Republics, the revolutionary poetic sensibility was strengthened by Neumann and Jaii Wolker. In their works, we find the grim struggle of the workers for social emancipation, the acute contradictions of capitalism and remnants of feudal social relations and the inevitable triumph of a new revolutionary social order. Neumann's *Red Sons* – a collection of poetry published in 1923 – and Wolker's *The Hour of Our Birth* – a collection of poetry published in 1922 – were significant expressions of this new revolutionary tendency in poetry. Commenting about the works of these two poets, D. Markov says:

> In the work of Neumann there is a marked predilection for political analysis and publicistic generalization. Wolker on the other hand, wrote poetry (directed by) emotions, had a flair for imaginative details and subtle psychological touches.[17]

Other Czech poets of this period worthy of mention are Josef Hora, Jaroslav Scifert and Vitezslav Nezual.

Bulgarian revolutionary poetic tradition of this period was championed by Khristo Smirnensky whose works such as the *Coal Miner* (1921) "presents an engrossing picture of the ... power of communist ideas that can spur on the masses of the working people to feats of revolutionary heroism." [18] In fact, Georgi Bakalov, a Bulgarian literary theorist and historian sees Smirnensky as the "stormy petrel of Bulgarian liberation."[19] Another poet of note of this period in Bulgaria is Geo Milev whose "September" (1924) in particular was so spectacular in its apprehension of the unflinching and unwavering striving of the masses for a new social order and its optimistic prophecy that "September will soon be May", suggestive of the triumph of proletarian class solidarity emblematic of the May Day – Workers' Day.

In Poland, Stanislaw Ryszard Stande, Witold Wandurski, Bruno Jasienski and Wladyslaw Broniewski solidified the revolutionary poetic tradition of the 19th century. Their poetry is dense with imagery that vibrates with the "violent anti-imperialist protest, with an angry exposure of those guilty of the tragic death of millions and calls for the revolutionary re-make of the world."[20] The positive response achieved by Broniewski's poetry is such that a fellow Polish critic, Wandurski, acknowledges him as a "revolutionary lyric poet, a lyric poet of great emotional powers."[21]

In Russia itself, many poets, most of them erstwhile idealistic symbolists and romantic futurists, turned their poetic craft towards the understanding of the new revolutionary order. Notable among these poets were Alexander Blok and Mayakovsky. Blok's "Twelve" – published in 1918 – captures the march of the masses which he likened to a fierce whirlwind. Mayakovsky's "V.I. Lenin" published in 1924 and *Fire* are significant signposts of post-revolution Russian revolutionary poetry. In the former, for example, he celebrates the determination of Lenin, the leader and inspirer of the Russian revolution.

The transition to revolutionary aesthetics in poetry from bourgeois romanticism is not always easy as shown in the case of Ivan Vazov, a Bulgarian poet of this period. The path of this transformation is always complex and contradictory and is conditioned, in the main, by the expansion of the social horizon and vision of the poet and his understanding of the revolutionary nature of society. Vazov has been a bitter critic of revolutionary poetry and thereby attracted adverse comments from progressive critics and literary aestheticians. But eventually, he progressed to a stage where his social vision is no longer antagonistic to revolutionary change. In response to this, Goergi Bakalov included some of his poetry in *Rays of Poetry*, an anthology of poetry he edited. Vosov's reaction to this development is this:

> Initially, my attitude to socialism was a hostile one, in as much as it seemed to be little more than a fashionable trend, which denied the importance of any other class than the proletariat. It is perfectly understandable why the socialists had harsh words for me after my early objections and used every opportunity to attack me, seeing in me an inveterate champion of the bourgeoisie. Now I see that their view of me has changed for me, poems on social issues make up a large part of Bakalov's anthology.[22]

S.K. Neumann, one of the revolutionary poets of this period who is equally a literary commentator of note, made some fundamental observations regarding the organic relationship between the commitment of the revolutionary poet to the cause of social change and his creative individuality and artistic independence. In that connection, he elucidates one of the significant aspects of the challenge of revolutionary art, when he opines that:

> Revolutionary idea of course demands discipline of the revolutionary writer. Yet the mature revolutionary system will not place restrictions on the writer of problems he treats. There are no contradictions in this. I would sum up this: In each work of a revolutionary writer, we are hoping to see a strong resolve to portray a character of a genuinely revolutionary type. That is our all important task...[23]

This observation is very imperative to the understanding of the direction of revolutionary aesthetics, the character of the revolutionary artist and the relationship between his social vision and artistic truth. The attainment of all these is as complex and difficult as the transition from bourgeois and petty-bourgeois ideo-aesthetic world view to revolutionary art, as the experience of Vazov demonstrates. It is not only in Eastern Europe that revolutionary poetry attained great height in the 1920s and beyond. In the period between 1920 and 1970, progressive poetry with deep and abiding revolutionary content and world view blossomed also in other parts of the world. In Western Europe for example, we have the example of Bertolt Brecht in Germany whose poetic creations are as intense and significant as his dramatic creations. Brecht sustained the tradition of revolutionary poetry for more than three decades in his homeland and used it as a means of instructing the masses, in analyzing the social condition, especially the contradictions inherent in capitalism, and in pointing at a revolutionary future as an inevitable consequence of historical dialectics. The simplicity of his diction, the concreteness of his imagery and the directness of his message, especially in such poems as "The Worker Talks to a Peasant" are as lively and historically true as his monumental work in creating the "Epic Theatre" in drama. Another poet of German origin worthy of mention in this context is J. Becher.

In France, Paul Eluard sustained this tradition and, in that connection, consistently shows the limitations of modernist poetry in its relation to revolutionary poetry. In Italy, this poetic tradition was sustained by poets such as Jorge Amado. In Chile, Pablo Neruda, one of the greatest poets of the 20th century and a Nobel Laureate in literature kept alive the flame of revolutionary poetry in his homeland and has inspired other revolutionary poets of Latin America and the Caribbean origin. In Turkey, Nazim Hikmet, who in the words of Orhan Seifi, has "shattered everything that was holy for us in art...,"[24] is particularly significant when we consider the development of revolutionary poetry in that country.

It is in realization of the gains of revolutionary poetry, its pride of place in the world literary process and its advantage over modernist abstraction, fragmentation and angst-filled naturalism that makes A. Ovcharenko say:

> We are overjoyed not only because many writers not only embraced revolutionary ideas but Gorky, Mayakovsky, A. Tolstoy, B. Brecht, J. Becher, L. Stoyanov, D. Dimov, L. Kruczkowski, T. Tuwim, H. Barbusse, Paul Eluard, Nazim Hikmet, Pablo Neruda and Jorge Amode took a strong revolutionary stand. In 1969 an interesting book was published here with a concrete, detailed account of a poetic renovation accomplished by Mayakovsky, Nezval, Hikmet and Neruda in the process of their conversion to revolutionary ideas.[24]

The history of revolutionary poetry is a continuous one. New historical phases and epochs generate impetuses from where the tradition finds substantial ideo-aesthetic basis of expression. Already in the 1930s, 1940s and 1950s, revolutionary poetic sensibility could be detected in African poetry, in the continent itself and in the Diaspora, but this will constitute the next part of our discourse. Suffice it to say that this sketchy overview of the socio-political context of the emergence and development of revolutionary poetry is enough indication and demonstration of the richness of revolutionary thought, and the consistent desire of progressive humanists to use poetry as a means of enriching the struggle of the working masses for a better world, without sacrificing the aesthetic basis of art itself.

Notes and References
1. Mao Tse-Tung, *Selected Works Vol. III* (Peking: Foreign Language Press, 1975), p. 81.
2. See, for example, A. Yegorov, "The Progressive Development of Art", in A. Zis, compl. *Problems of Contemporary Aesthetics* (Moscow: Progress, 1984)

where this point is clearly made and substantiated. The article also has Karl Marx's oft-quoted assertion that Greek art, despite being a product of the nascent stage in the evolution of world civilization, still generates incomparable interest in industrial societies.
3. This issue of literature having a dialectical relationship with ideology has been investigated by such scholars as Pierre Marcharey (The Theory of Literary Production); Louis Althusser, (For Marx and "Literature and Ideological State Apparatuses"); Lucien Goldmann (The Hidden God, Methods in the Sociology of Literature and Toward a Sociology of the Novel); Raymond Williams (Marxism and Literature) and Terry Eagleton (Criticism and Ideology).
4. B.M. Boguslavsky, et al. *ABC of Dialectical and Historical Materialism* (Moscow: Progress Publishers, 1975), p. 32.
5. S.S. Prawer, *Karl Marx and World Literature.* Oxford: Oxford Univesity Press, 1976, pp. 67-68.
6. Karl Marx, Friedrich Engels, Wreck. Herouisgegeber Von Institute for Marxismus-Leninimus beim 2k der SED (Berlin, 195-69); quoted in Prawer's *Karl Marx and World Literature*
7. *Karl Marx and World Literature*, pp. 67-68.
8. Ibid., p. 68
9. Ibid., pp.60-75
10. D. Markov, *Socialist Literatures: Problems of Development* (Moscow: Progress, 1984), p. 19.
11. Karl Marx and F. Engels, *Collected Works, Vol. 21* (Moscow: Progress, 1964), p. 21 Quoted in *Socialist Literatures*, p. 19.
12. Socialist Literatures, p. 19.
13. V.I. Lenin, *Collected Works, Vol. 36,* p. 224. Quoted in *Socialist Literatures,* p.19.
14. *Socialist Literatures,* p. 22.
15. Ibid., p. 22.
16. Ibid., p. 25.

17. Ibid., p. 44.
18. Ibid., p. 46.
19. Georgi Bakalov, *Selected Works, Vol. 2* (Sofia: Pisatel Press, 1963), p. 19.
20. *Socialist Literatures*, p.47
21. W. Wandurski, "From Legions to Revolution", Foreword to the book, W. Broniewski, *Selected Verse, 1923-1931* (Moscow, 1932), p. 3.
22. Ivan Vazov, *Collected Works in 20 Volumes* (Sofia: Bulgarsky Pistel Publishers, 1957), p. 149.
23. S.K. Neumann, *Selected Works,* (Moscow, 1953), p.302
24. See *Socialist Realism and the Modern Literary Process* (Moscow: Nvosti Press, 1978).
25. *Socialist Realism*, pp. 269-270. The book in question is *The Poetry of Socialism, a Collection* (Moscow, 1969).

Part Two

GENESIS OF ART AND IDEOLOGY IN AFRICAN POETRY: NEGRITUDE AND NATIONALIST POETRY

It is imperative to make certain clarificatory statements from the onset in order to make very clear and straightforward our position. Art and ideology are not only colonial or postcolonial aesthetic modes and forms of artistic expression. This is a reality as old as all societies in Africa. In basing our discussion on colonial and postcolonial poetic expressions, we are only substantiating the fact that these periods are very cogent and decisive in the overall context of the African experience. Colonial social formation and the postcolonial social system it engendered and conditioned are processes that lie at the base of reality-apprehension and mediation by most African creative writers. Their impetuses, nevertheless, embrace pre-colonial structures of thought and social reality, but their exploration of experience is substantially based on modern sensibility over-determined by colonial and postcolonial social, cultural and aesthetic imperatives. A thorough-going dialectical study, thus, has to be deeply rooted on a historical continuum that encompasses the pre-colonial, but which will take the discussion beyond the boundary of written art to accommodate art and ideological forms generated by societies that produced them. It is therefore, to restrict our discussion to the African contemporary experience and to underscore the specific poetic responses to colonial imperialism and postcolonial existentialist traumas that we have to base our discussion on modern African poetry.

Secondly, the discussion follows the pattern of conventional and essentially Eurocentric critical scholarship by limiting discussion to "Africa South of the Sahara", not because of a lack of an alternative radical demarcatory system but for reasons quite different from those advanced by conservative scholars. This could be put simply thus: even though colonial imperialism is a reality in virtually all countries of Africa, North African countries are, nevertheless, concretely placed in the mainstream for freedom struggle located the emancipator possibility of the combination of radical Islamism and socialism: Egypt (under Nasser), Libya (under Gaddafi) Algeria (under Ben Bella), etc.

Moreover, these countries never experienced cultural deracination that bothers on a compulsive loss of any sustaining belief and crisis of consciousness the way "Sub-Saharan" African countries did. These countries are therefore unique in their near complete loss of organic contact with the pre-Islamic past (contingent encounters are evident only) and a failure to come to a wholesome grip with the present (substantially mutilated and distorted by colonial ethos and that sporadic incursions into the past). The difference between Islamic North Africa and the rest of the continent is more cultural and ideological than geographical and linguistic. It is this ideo-cultural particularism that conditions the difference between the sensibilities of poets of these areas.

A study of art and ideology of "Sub-Saharan" Africa will lead materialist reading of Africa-Western imperialism dialectic, while a scrutiny of North African poetry will lead to influences beyond the colonial encounter and postcolonial predicament, to a discourse on the nature of Islam as an ideo-aesthetic category. This will be beyond the scope of the present effort, though it is an area worth exploring.

Finally, the then peculiar apartheid formation in South Africa has produced poetry whose artistic form and ideological structure are substantially different from what we find in West and East Africa. As a specific and somewhat unique expression of colonial authority, apartheid was separated from conventional colonial imperialism by its distinct inner racial logic and dialectic. For this very reason, politics and poetry in South Africa are treated separately in this discourse. This is also to enable us to contextualize and place revolutionary poetic response to apartheid in its proper socio-historical and socio-aesthetic matrix.

This section on the genesis of art and ideology in African poetry is treated in two parts: Negritude poetry which is essentially a Francophone Africa phenomenon and the amorphous "Nationalist" poetry which is predominantly an Anglophone Africa phenomenon.

Negritude Poetry: Francophone Africa

Negritude or Black affirmation was a poetic movement initiated by Aime Cesaire, a black West Indian in his *Return to My Native Land* in 1939, as a conscious attempt to assess not only Black identity and socio-cultural essence but also to project a revolutionary dimension of Negritude poetry as different from its interpretation by elitist scholars like Wole Soyinka and Lewis Nkosi[1] who see it as a homological ideology without inner contradictions. Revolutionary scholarship on the other hand, has distinguished two main, contradictory directions of the movement: the revolutionary affirmative direction of writers like Cesaire and David Diop and the quasi-mystical and romantic affirmative direction of writers like Leopold Sedar Senghor. The first places black consciousness in its firm socio-historical context and approaches the issue of the challenge to French (Western) cultural and political domination from a consistent materialist and dialectical position while the latter, which is essentially idealistic, predetermine pre-colonial and anti-colonial experience as a mystical, romantic ontological category that lacks objective and materialist standpoint.

Before we can correctly elucidate the significance of Negritude as a historical phenomenon and ideo-aesthetic imperative, it will be pertinent to take a cursory look at the socio-historical and socio-political reality to which it is a response. French colonial socio-cultural policy was a programmed and phased attempt to erase authentic and original African ideals through the assimilation of Africans into the mainstream French post-enlightenment bourgeois civilization. Rejecting the African world as a non-reality, the French colonialists sought to implant in the colonized the Greco-Roman precepts of individualism, free enterprise and other cultural and political values that are distinctly Western. The extremity of this programme, the enthusiasm and zeal with which it was carried out and the determination and commitment of its enforcers led to an extremist reaction from emergent black intellectuals in the French colonial dependencies. This extreme reaction took the form of conscious assertion of the validity and genuineness of Black pre-colonial civilization and identity formation and a rejection of the imposed Western metaphysical world view. As already pointed out, the affirmation of black identity and ethos took the specific forms of, on the one hand, a historically rooted materialist-revolutionary dimension, and, on the other hand, a pseudo-mystical and quasi-cultural dimension. Omafume Onoge, a revolutionary literary scholar, puts this beautifully when he asserts that:

> ...the affirmative consciousness which typified Negritude contained two tendencies right from the inception of the movement. These two tendencies which, initially, were merely divergent, are today quite opposed. They are the revolutionary affirmation associated with Cesaire, and the mystical affirmation associated with Senghor... A consequence of this

inability to separate the variants of negritude is an undifferentiating acceptance or rejection of the Negritude movement, by commentators since Sartre celebrated it in his Orphee Noir. For example, the movement in its entirety has been hailed either as the intellectual origins of the African revolution (Kesteloot) or indicated as irrelevant 'escapist narcissism' (Soyinka and others).[2]

Onoge further correctly argues that the "dialectical triad" which conditions Cesaire's standpoint are:

> Thesis (sovereignty, harmony and glory of pre-colonial Africa), anti-thesis (colonial alienation, political, economic and cultural oppression because of colonialism), synthesis (acceptance of pre-colonial heritage, removal of colonialism).[3]

David Diop, a follower of Cesaire and one of the 'revolutionary affirmative' poets, demonstrates this dialectical view of African history in his poems 'Africa' and 'The Vulture'. In them, he shows an awareness of historical processes and a readiness to interpret African historical experience from the materialist standpoint. His 'Africa' follows Cesaire's line of argument about the thesis-antithesis-synthesis dialectic for the poem schematizes African history into its three main stages of development: pre-colonial epoch of glory and freedom, colonial subjugation and loss of identity, and independence which is an assertion of self will and a restoration of pre-colonial harmony. Parts of the poem read thus, with each corresponding to the above structural framework:

1. Pre-Colonial glory
   Africa my Africa
   Africa of proud warriors in the ancestral Savannahs,
   Africa my grandmother sings of

2. Colonial Oppression
   Your black blood spilt over the fields

>   The blood of your sweat
>   The toil of slavery
>   The slavery of your children
>
> 3. Assertion of Independence
>   That tree that grows....
>   Is Africa, your Africa. It puts forth new shoots
>   With patience and stubbornness puts forth new shoots
>
>   Slowly its fruits grow to have
>   The bitter taste of liberty.⁴

In 'The Vulture', just as in 'Africa', Diop demonstrates his understanding of African historical and political development and the ruthless nature of French colonial imperialism which, pretending innocence, actually destroys every bit of humanity in the African. As in the other poem, Diop recognizes the African capacity of endurance and struggle and projects a revolutionary future of freedom and liberty. He schematizes the dialectic of suppression and revolt thus:

> 1. Christian Hypocrisy and Colonial Violence
>   In those days
>   When civilization kicked us in the face
>   When holy water slapped our cringing brows
>   The vultures built in the shadow of their talons
>   The bloodstained monument of tutelage.
>
> 2. Imperialist Deception
>   O the bitter memories of extorted kisses
>   Of promises broken at the point of a gun
>   Of foreigners who did not seem human
>   Who knew all the books but did not know love
>
> 3. Imperative of Revolutionary Consciousness
>   In spite of your songs of pride
>   In spite of the desolate villages of torn Africa

> Hope was preserved in us as in a fortress
> And from the mines of Swaziland to the factories
> of Europe
> Spring will be reborn under our bright steps.[5]

Aime Cesaire himself, the founder of the revolutionary school of Negritude poetry, has demonstrated convincingly in his poetry that only a total uprooting of colonial imperialism and its replacement by Progressive People's Republics in all the colonial dominions can save the black world from cultural and socio-political annihilation. He is thoroughly aware of the ravages of colonialism which he captures thus:

> Neither the teacher in his classroom
> Nor the priest at Catechism can get a single word from
> this half asleep child...
> for his voice has lost its mind in the marshes of hunger
> and there is nothing, nothing to be got from the little
> good-for-nothing, nothing but hunger which can no
> longer climb the tackle of his voice a heavy, flabby
> hunger a hunger buried in the deepest heart of the
> Hunger of the famished Morne.[6]

But Cesaire is also aware of the temporality of white colonial domination, its transitory nature in the context of social development and the inevitable triumph of positive nationalism. He captures this process lucidly in the same sequences of poems in *Return to my Native land*:

> Listen to the white world appallingly weary from its
> immense effort the crack of its joints rebelling under
> the hardness of the stars listen to the proclaimed
> victories which trumpet their defeats.[7]

Aime Cesaire's entire literary and intellectual career is conditioned by his consistent and unflinching demand for equality of the black man in his relation with other people, but this demand is never made in the purely racist sense of inherent racial binary opposition or contradiction but in the recognition that historical imperatives – and they are not eternal – determine the condition of the black man. His call for social amelioration is therefore an ideological and political call, and not a racist one. Even in his collection, *Cahier*, where he registers the anger and defiance of the slave, we hear the latter narrating the historical temporalities on which his torture and victimization lie. For example, his subjugation is based on this premise of negation:

> Those who did not invent gun powder nor compass
> Those who never controlled stream non electricity
> Those who explored neither water nor sky (p.68)

But notwithstanding the above European consciousness in its relation with the African world, which consists of the African mind with its all-creative and reflexive potentialities, we know that "those who never explored the sky and the water" nevertheless:

> ... Knew in their deepest parts within,
> The country of suffering
> Knew of no voyage except when uprooted (p. 68)

These dialectical images of oppression counterpoised to defiance and suppression and colonial rape counterpoised to liberation and revolutionary triumph are recurring motifs in Cesaire's works, whether in the poetry collections *Ferrements* (1960), *Cadastre* (1961) and *Les Armes Miraculeuses* (1946) or in his plays *Et Les Chiens se Taisaient* (1956), *Une Saison du Congo* (1966) and *La Tragedie du Rio Christophe* (1963), the last two mediating the reactionary conspiracy against Patrice Lumumba of Congo and the tragedy of King Christopher of the West Indies respectively. In his intellectual productions also, Cesaire unhesitatingly exposes the romantic interpretation of African history, culture, anthropology and philosophy and posits a materialist argument against it. In discourse on colonialism, he challenges imperialists' assumptions about African past and present and sees the academia as an extension of the debilitating arm of colonial atavism and culture of annihilation. In a brilliant analysis of Cesaire's argument in the book, Onoge posits:

> In the Discourse on Colonialism, a document which reveals his enormous familiarity with the ethnographic literature of the time, no anthropological report, no matter how liberal, evades the colonial presence, and engages, instead in idealist interpretations of African culture, receives approval. Thus Cesaire saw the intrinsic dishonesty of Reverend Placide Tempels' celebrated discovery of the 'vital forces' of Bantu philosophy. The theme of 'vital forces' which later forms the cornerstone of Senghor's outlook and other studies of African philosophy, was, for Cesaire, another instance of anthropology in the service of imperialism.[8]

Cesaire is not alone in projecting the revolutionary affirmation of Negritude. Though in Africa he has been overshadowed by Senghor principally because of the long reign of Eurocentric critical scholarship in African literature and the deliberate attempt by the products of this tradition to stifle revolutionary literature, he has influenced a number of artists, cultural workers and political activists considerably, especially in the Francophone African countries. We have already given the example of David Diop who is one of the purveyors of this revolutionary alternative. In prose fiction, too, the works of Mongo Beti, Ferdinand Oyono and Sembene Ousmane, are remarkable demonstrations of the revolutionary potentials of Negritude as a liberating phenomenon. In the words of Onoge:

> It is this revolutionary affirmative consciousness that we can creditably attribute to Cesaire's concept of Negritude. He was not without followers. In the body of African literature in French, usually labeled as Negritude, we can see hints that at certain phases

of their artistic careers, the withering satire of Mongo Beti and Ferdinand Oyono, the revolutionary advocacy and optimism of David Diop, were in the tradition of Cesaire.[9]

If we realize that Mongo Beti had not yet published *Perpetua and the Habit of Unhappiness* and Remember Reuben, and Sembene Ousmane had not yet published *Xala* and *The Last of the Empire* when Onoge made this postulation, we can begin to appreciate the solidity of his insight, the concreteness of his prediction and the relevance of his historically rooted study and research.

In the introduction of *Marxism and African Literature*, Georg M. Gugelberger says:

> To do so (charting 'alternative terrain' for the African literary situation)... It was necessary to come to terms with one of Africa's most outstanding literary figures, one who presently seems to hold (at least in the bourgeois world) a position only Leopold Senghor held before him: Wole Soyinka.[10]

This indirect comment on Senghor more than any other thing summarizes for us the significance and centrality of Senghor in African literature and the degree of his appreciation in the Western world. Senghor has come to be associated with Negritude and despite the scathing comments of Soyinka, Nkosi and Mphahlele, is seen as the embodiment of that essentially progressive tradition. A true understanding of the poetry of Senghor, nevertheless, must take cognizance of his expressed symbiotic and hybridized status as a cultural half-caste or bastard; his idealistic and romantic conception of the African past; his mystical exploration of African ontology and cosmological system; and his ahistorical understanding of the African social dynamics and process of revolutionary transformation.

Senghor is more interested in his exploration of the "vital forces" of primordial Africa, a philosophical belief which he borrows from Tempels and Kagame and which depicts the

African world in its supposed innocence and undiluted infancy. His poem "Black Woman" reads thus:

> Naked Woman, black woman
> Clothed with your colour which is life, with your form
> Which is beauty!
> In your shadow I have grown up; the gentleness of
> Your hands was laid over my eyes
> And now, high up on the sun-baked pass, at the heart of
> summer, at the heart of noon, I come upon you, my
> Promised land.
> And your beauty strikes me to the heart like the flash
> of an eagle.[11]

And so the other stanzas continue. Fully aware of the horrors of imperialism and its destruction of the very essence and being of the African, Senghor finds escape and solace in mystical shamanism, in effusive sentimentality, in idealism and amorphous romanticism. In his poems, such as the one above, the breeze is always flapping the palms in the homestead, the night sky is lit with moony brilliance and elders gather late at night to tell tales. Naked women display their beauty and the sounds of night birds add candor and mystery to the magic of the moment. His idea of colonialism as a historical phenomenon is cultural and not political and economic. In Onoge's words:

> With Senghor, the taming of the revolutionary potential of Negritude becomes complete. Given his preoccupation with the politics of identity, his theory of colonialism is strictly cultural. The colonial situation is diagnosed essentially as a cultural encounter between Africa and Europe. Senghor, as far as we know, has nowhere advanced a systematic critique of the colonial order in terms of economic exploitation.[12]

In his poem dealing with the ancestors, understood by him as forlorn voices of a bygone ancient time, creating a living awareness in him through the instrumentality of the "vital forces", we detect the same wistful note of wonder, the same idyllic and nostalgic, illusory and fleeting cultural image, and the same torturous attempt to come to grip with an ideal lost in the abyss of time:

> Listen to the voice of the Ancestors of Elissa.
> Like us exiled
> They did not wish to die, to lose their seminal
> Flow in dust
> Let me listen too in the smoky hut for the
> Phantom visit of propitious souls....
> Let me breathe the smell of our
> Dead ones, let me recall and repeat their
> Living accents, let me learn
> To live before I go down, deeper than the diver,
> Into the deep darkness of sleep.[13]

In his analysis of the fantastic and unreal image of an African past calling to an unknown cultural presence, one of the major voices of Eurocentric critical scholarship in Africa, O.R. Dathorne, says:

> Though he was Westernized and had been taught of the eternal permanence of matter, his African instincts, in addition, continuously assured him of the indestructible spirit of man. What Senghor is therefore attempting is for him the obvious – the Vital Force in everything, which Fr. Plaude Tempels and Alexis Kagame have also written.[14]

O.R. Dathorne, like Senghor, subscribes to the obscurantist belief that reason is essentially an European attribute, while instinct, emotion and passion are African essence; that the technology of Europe is counterbalanced by the primeval and instinctual vital force of Africa. In accepting this colonialist and dependencist paradigm, Senghor and the Eurocentric critical campaigners of his works, accept a slave status rationalized only on the parameter of the total irreversibility of the colonial situation; find accommodation under the umbrella of cultural symbiosis and hybridity; are lured by the hope in the inevitability of the European presence and are seduced by a forlorn prayer for the salvation of imperialist brigands for their sins against Africa.

It is Senghor whose theory of positive acculturation states thus:

> I think all the great civilizations resulted from an interbreeding, objectively speaking – Indian Civilization, Greek Civilization, French Civilization, etc, etc.

In my opinion, and objectively, this interbreeding is necessary. It is a result of the contact of civilizations.[15]

It is equally the same Senghor who on the eve of Senegalese independence (awarded because of the assurance that French colonial interests will be protected in neo-colonial Senegal by Senghor) defines and interprets for us the significance of France in world politics and culture:

> On the economic level France can get along without Black Africa, but she cannot get along without it on the political or cultural place. France is not Holland. She is a great lady who needs to spread her radiance over a large family. Reduced to her European dimensions, she would fail in her mission to the world, which is to defend Man: She would lose her soul and raison d'etre."[16]

It is also the same Senghor who above separates, codifies and mutually opposes politics, culture and economics to each other as self-contained wholes; and who argues that the solution to the crisis of colonialism and white economic, political and cultural predation on Africa is "not the total rejection of the white world and acceptance of the African world, but the blending of both". Finally, it is the same Senghor who, in "Prayer for Peace II" implores "Lord, God, forgive White Europe" when he assures us that they have made

My household servants into 'boys', my peasants into
Wage-earners, my people into a working class for
Thou must forgive those who have hunted my
children like wild elephants, and broken them in with
whips, have made them the black hands of those
whose hands were white. For Thou must forgive
those who exported ten millions of my sons in the
leper houses of their ships. Who killed two hundred
millions of them Lord, the glasses of my eyes grow
dim and lo, the serpent of hatred raises its head in
my heart, that serpent that I believed was dead. Kill
it Lord, for I must follow my way, and I would pray
especially for France.[17]

The list is endless; Senghor's own brand of Negritude is laden with inherent contradictions simply because of the contradictions of Senghor the man, the politician and the bourgeois nationalist.

When Sartre wrote about those Africans who were especially handpicked to be branded with the Greco-Roman precepts of individualism and free enterprise in Europe and America and who came back to their people with empty gluttonous words which mean nothing'[18] he was talking about the likes of Senghor. The history of Senegal since flag independence is an eloquent testimony of the emptiness of Senghor's Negritude and the emptiness, too, of his cultural symbiosis. Suffused with magical images and appeal to primordial and instinctual "vital forces"; deeply rooted in romantic idealism and mystical epiphany; and acutely lacking in historical consciousness, Senghor's Negritude is a far cry from the "revolutionary affirmative consciousness", to use Onoge's term, which informs the writings of Cesaire and David Diop. Its apologetic tone, its pitiful desire to please, placate and forgive, and its appeal to an abstract universal brotherhood which is reducible in the long run to Western particularistic world view are all indices of the innate contradictions of his firm commitment to Pax Europa.

In conclusion, therefore, we can confidently assert that

the critical confusion which Negritude engendered is predicated on the inability of African scholars to understand the contradictory nature of that ideo-aesthetic phenomenon and their incapacity to differentiate the revolutionary and romantic tendencies in it. By lumping together the whole of Negritude movement as a holistic or monolithic phenomenon, most critics end up making sweeping historical statements about it. Soyinka's charge that a tiger need not proclaim his "tigritude", Lewis Nkosi's argument that "one sees in these poems and stories the implications of a literary ideology which may be as crippling to young writers as the high-handed dictates of a cultural commissar in communist countries"[19] and Eskia Mphahiele's opinion that Negritude is "sheer romanticism, often it is Mawkish and strikes a pose"[20] are samples of this undifferentiated critical observations. So is John Povey's positive comment that "it demonstrated that poetry and literature were not only possible in the African manner and out of an African attitude of mind, but that only such poetry was legitimate."[21]

It is only a thorough-going materialist study of the movement – which lay bare the hidden political and cultural motives of the practitioners – that can correctly apprehend the artistic form and ideological structures of Negritude. In short, a study of art and ideology in Negritude poetry cannot be separated from the socio-historical, socio-political and socio-cultural contexts of colonial imperialism which gave the movement its initial imperative and which served as subjects for Negritudinist reaction. It is only this mode of critical intervention that can espouse the revolutionary articulation of reality by Cesaire and others, and the mystic-cultural pretensions of Senghor and his followers.

'Nationalist' Poetry: Anglophone Africa

There are a lot of assumptions about 'nationalist' poetry. For one, it is adjudged as the counterpart of Negritude poetry which is essentially a French-African phenomenon. Secondly, it is believed that the poems lack artistic finesse, and are mainly superficial poeticization of the burning socio-political issues of the day. Thirdly, the 'nationalist' poets are generally seen as "professional" politicians and public figures whose training do not qualify or prepare them for any serious poetic composition of considerable aesthetic edification and artistic intensity.

Despite the critical efforts of scholars to subject these poems to close analytical study, little attempts have been made to see them from the ideo-aesthetic perspective. The limitation of past researches in the field is predicated on the unwillingness or incapacity of scholars to see that phenomenon as a product of colonial imperialism and the poets as constituting a class in emergent African states.

'Nationalist' poetry, roughly believed to have emerged, developed and degenerated between 1927–1957, is a movement which has such people as Gladys Casely-Hayford, Raphael Ernest Grail Armattoe, Dennis Chukwude Osadebay, Michael Dei-Annang and Nnamdi Azikiwe as the major voices. It is important to locate the handicaps of these poets not only on the formal, structural and artistic levels, as some scholars will want us to believe,[22] but also on the ideological level. Most of these poets were elitist nationalists who used the poetic form to give vent to their idea of the governance of the polity, to express their feelings and standpoint on colonial imperialism and national independence, to defend the humanity of the black man and to appeal to the world about the necessity of accommodation, brotherhood and universal fraternity. Taking all these declared sentiments as given and manifest, few critics bother to search deeper into the objective, concretely existing socio-political beliefs of these poets. They fail to appreciate the fact that these poets, being essentially elitist nationalists, with all the contradictions and vacillations of their class, did not, in fact, call for the systematic dislocation of colonial imperialism, the negation of Western values and the establishment of truly independent and revolutionary postcolonial governments in Africa.

GENESIS OF ART AND IDEOLOGY IN AFRICAN ... ■ 53

Dennis Osadebay is one example of a poet tortured by his native conscience to recognize the yearnings of Africans for a continent free from the ruthless clutches of imperialism and colonial rape, but who also sends heartfelt felicitations to Britain for civilizing his continent. On the one hand, we detect the prophetic plea for justice and hope embodied in the restlessness of African youth and masses, and on the other, the uninhibited, praise of the colonizers. "Who Buys My Thoughts" represents the first tendency while "Thank You Sons and Daughters of Britannia" the second. In the former poem, we hear:

> Who buys my thoughts
> Buys not a cup of honey
> That sweetens every taste;
> He buys the throb
> Of young Africa's soul
> The soul of teerning millions,
> Hungry, naked, sick
> Yearning, pleading, waiting
>
> Who buys my thoughts
> Buys the spirit of the age,
> The unquenching fire that smolders
> And smolders
> In every living heart
> That's true and noble or suffering:
> It burns all o'er the heart
> Destroying, chastening, cleansing[23]

It is the same Osadebay who in a later poem which appeared in the collection *African Sings* published in 1952 wrote:

> Thank you
> Sons and daughters of Britannia
> You gave me hospitals
> You gave me schools
> Thank you
> Yours is the happiness of giving

The joy of doing good (p.14)

Osadebay is unable to understand the contradiction in his art and ideological position because of his hybridized status as a defender of European values and a campaigner for African dignity and independence. He fails to see that despite the "schools and hospitals" built by the imperialists, that the "teeming millions of his people are still "hungry, naked, sick" to use his own very expression. His art is, therefore, as contradictory as his political and ideological loyalty, as contradictory as his fight for "independence", and his insistence that the social formation determined by colonial imperialism should remain substantially unchanged even after "independence" is won.

The ideo-aesthetic problem encountered by Osadebay because of his cultural hybridism, ambivalent identity and 'double loyalty' to African nationalism and British imperialism is also encountered by the other "nationalist" poets, like Gladys Casely-Hayford, who was not even as politically committed to the nationalist struggle as Osadebay. A careful reading of her works will reveal the same intense contradictions that are inherent in Osadebay's art.

She is surely aware of her role as a moral force and an advocate of justice and racial equality. But she is also a Christian, a believer in the doctrine of spiritual salvation according to the spiritual imperatives of the oppressor. While on the one hand, she urges Africans to rejoice for being made black, she still recreates the birth of Christ, even though she gives it a local colouring and African touch. The point of emphasis here is that her localization of Christ to a specific African domain is not the denial of his whiteness, but a romantic delusion about something that ought to be but is not. Christ should have been born black, but was not; hence the attempt to wish away his historical origin and primogeniture. There does not exist for Hayford any equal historical and religious figure that could be recreated in poetic form for the instruction of his people. There is no

Shaka, no Sundiatta, nor the numerous priests and custodians of oracles in Africa that are worthy of artistic focus; it must be an iconic figure with a white background, because that world is very real and ever present in her imagination and consciousness. In the first poem, we read:

> Rejoice and shout with laugher
> Throw all your burdens down
> If God has been so gracious
> As to make you black or brown
> For you are great nations
> A people of great birth
> For where would spring the flowers
> If God took away the earth?
> Rejoice and shout with laughter
> Throw all your burdens down
> Yours is a glorious heritage
> *If you are black, or brown*[24]

Part of the second poem about Christ goes thus:
> Within a native hut, ere stirred the dawn,
> Unto the Pure One was an infant born,
> Wrapped in blue lappah, that As mother dyed,
> Laid on His father's home-tanned deer skin hide
> The Babe still slept, by all things glorified
> Spirits of black bards burst their bonds"[25]
> And sang 'Peace upon earth' until the heavens rang.

On a careful reading, one even notices that even in the first poem which celebrates the joy in being black, no solution is proffered to the numerous social-political and socio-economic problems engendered by colonial imperialism. Africans are simply advised to "Throw their burdens down" and rejoice for the mere fact of being black. Being black does not entail fighting in the jungles, enduring all forms of humiliation and racial inequality; it does not entail participation in protest marches and labour stoppages, in civil disobedience and sabotage against imperialism and its local agents. It simply means laughter and joy. One notices that the colonial factor must have been a constant reminder to Hayford about the necessity of art and its true propaganda potentials, for it was a period of intense upheavals and national awakening, of the grim determination of African peoples to liberate themselves from the social cannibalism of imperialism. As for the second poem, little need be said except that it illustrates the dilemma of the elitist class in its attempt to accommodate two contradictory world views, two ideological outlooks that are mutually opposed: the world of authentic ontology of being genuinely African in its realization of the revolutionary dynamics of society of which it is a part, and the world imperialism with its stifling political, economic, socio cultural and religious institutions. This dilemma transfigures into a tragic reality because of the incapacity of Hayford and her likes to adapt to either of the two worlds comfortably or accept their ontological essences.

O.R. Dathorne sees R.E.G. Armattoe as a poet whose dualism of vision (firm commitment to African fight for freedom, and his anti-racial stance that ridicules the stupidities of his fellow Africans) is expressed in the poet's word that "it is the responsibility of the African poet 'to know his past and express that past in authentic and unmistakable accents' as well as write without a conscious appeal in any racial context".[26] His collection of poems, *Between the Forest and the Sea* was published in 1950 while *Deep Down the Black Man's Mind* was published in 1954, a year after his death. The poems in these collections show his awareness of the reality of imperialism and the African challenge to it and the betrayal of the African revolution by some of his compatriots who see everything good about Europe. With regard to the last named tendency in his works, and observing that he wrote most of his poems in the 1940s, one is at a loss in understanding what makes Raskhan say the following things about Armattoe:

> This poet has great faith in the Negro race in general

and vast visions and plans for it as a race. But when he considers the activities of particular black men in politics and in the running of their country, he is rightly or wrongly so disappointed that he lashes out at his beloved black race with serpentine fury".[27]

For one, no West African country had won 'flag independence'; that is, attained postcolonial status by the 1940s with the exception of the unique situation of Liberia; no appreciable African participation in government was even felt at that period. In Nigeria, for example, it was the Richards Constitution of 1946 and the Littleton Constitution of 1954 (all after Armattoe must have ceased writing as a poet) that gave Africans any marginal say in colonial administration. Ghana won its independence in 1957, Guinea in 1958, Nigeria in 1960 and most other countries between 1960 and 1964. One, therefore, wonders who were the blacks "running their ... country" then, that Armattoe castigated, as Raskhan wants us to understand? It is doubly surprising too because Raskhan who is a contemporary of Armattoe (his article was published in 1957) should have known otherwise. Had the article appeared in the 1960s, one would have concluded that Raskhan deliberately mistook Armattoe for the emergent critical realist poets like Okigbo, Okot P'Bitek, J.P. Clark-Bekederemo and Wole Soyinka who really castigated the inheritors of power after 'flag independence'. But Raskhan's article came out in 1957 (Feb.-March), before Ghana even gained her independence and a good four years after the death of Armattoe. We, therefore, wonder who Raskhan was writing about with regard to Armattoe's poetry.

What Armattoe did within the limit of his critical realist consciousness is to satirize those Africans who collaborated with the whites in oppressing their people, who bought all the arguments of imperialism and hated everything African. His message is to the "home guards," the reactionary native elites, the treacherous politicians masquerading as nationalist leaders and the zealous and enthusiastic evangelical Christians destroying African spiritual and religious heritage even before the white master gave the order. The poem that brings out all these things forcefully is "Servant Kings".

> Leave them alone
> Leave them to be
> Man lost to shame
> To honour lost!
> Servant-Kinglets,
> Riding to war
> Against their own,
> Watched by their foes
> Who urge them on
> And laugh at them!
> Leave them alone
> Man lost to shame,
> To honour lost.[28]

Despite Armattoe's critical disposition towards imperialism and its local agents, his poetry still reveals the same ideo-aesthetic weaknesses manifest in the works of the other 'nationalist' poets. Some of his works like "The Lonely Soul," "Little Child", "Africa" and "The Way I Would Like to Die", all found in the collection *Deep Down the Black Man's Mind*, are escapist and illusory. In them he reveals an unwillingness or even incapacity to come to concrete grips with the socio-historical processes of his time. He hesitates to make categorical poetic statements about the events of the day, and instead finds solace in privatist thoughts couched as public statements. His vision, like the vision of his contemporaries, is a split vision, a vision of self contradiction and indirection, occasioned by his class-bound willingness to help the people but a realization that he is incapable of doing that.

Another poet of this period worthy of mention is the Ghanaian, Michael Dei-Anang. With three published collections, *Wayward Lines from Africa* (1946) *Cocoa Comes to Mamphong* (1949) and *Two Faces of Africa* (1965), he established himself as a poet worthy of serious consideration, at least from the socio-historical and socio-aesthetic perspectives. Like the other poets of the period, he is interested in the awakening consciousness of new Africa and the gradually developing sensibility of a people on the threshold of re-affirming their spiritual worth and collective heritage. As he said in 'A Writer's Outlook': "I sing of Africa because I know her best. I am proud of her beauty, music and folklore, because these come nearest to my heart".[29]

Like these other poets, too, his world outlook is replete with contradictions and broken visions, with a torturous attempt to capture the intensity of the milieu and the sublimation of aesthetic consciousness into the realms of myth, legend, fantasy and romance. On the face of it, one may assume that his concern with Africa is a progressive stance, but a deeper scrutiny of his art reveals an inability to relate African past-conceived as a harmonious social order – with the turbulent contemporary epoch. When the proper socio-historical context of his poetic compositions (1946–1965) is revealed as a medley of imperialist repression and the nationalist resistance to it, and the betrayal of the emancipatory hopes and re-humanizing possibilities of postcoloniality by the emergent black ruling class, his escapism becomes glaring. In "Dear Africa", for instance, he urges African people thus:

> Awake, though sleeping heart!
> Awake, and kiss
> The love-lorn brow
> Of this ebony lass,
> Dear Africa,
> Whose virgin charms
> Ensnare the love-lit hearts
> Of venturing Youth
> From another lands.[30]

It is very clear that Dei-Anang is not addressing Africa struggling to rediscover itself after centuries of colonial rape and imperialist plunder. He is not speaking to freedom fighters battling the reactionary forces in the jungles; neither is he talking to the restless African working people combating the pressures of living under the colonial establishment. He is addressing an abstraction, an ideal, a child of his thought and imagination. He is addressing a "virgin" Africa of "sleeping lions", unconscious yet of her situatedness in the context of historical progression and human transformation.

This historical view of Africa, devoid of relevant social content, is the standard form of universalizing a reality to accommodate thoughts and opinions alien to a specific environment in a clearly defined historical time. It dispenses with contextual variables and specificities of place and moment and projects an amorphous vision of eternal verities that survive the ravages of fundamental historical changes. This pursuit of eternal values as against the exposition of particular socio-historical situations reaches a high degree of intensity in "Let's Live in Peace" in which Dei-Anang discovers suddenly that strife, stress, upheavals and national agitations – of which violence and deaths are essential parts – pay nobody, the colonialist or the nationalist. Every vestige of social disorder has to be wiped out for the harmonious existence of all classes and races in society. It is as if he wants to wish history away; the complex dialectic of a social formation (colonial imperialism and national dependency) which determines the contest of power between two groups whose interests are diametrically opposed, and whose triumph must be predicated on the context of deliberate violence unleashed by the hegemonic forces and the counter-hegemony incarnated by the colonial and postcolonial subalterns.

Despite centuries of social barbarization of Africans, the solution to the African dilemma is not in meting out righteous violence in equal measure, but respecting the eternal injunctions of brotherhood, piety and social compromise. The poem reads:

> Where the rivers of time
> Are fouled by native stress and strife,
> And man becomes his own enemy,
> Life is distraught
> And its colourful scenes
> Are marred and stained violent
> By dark-brown blot of blood
> Let's live in peace
> For here, like tenants
> In thatched huts, we dwell
> Soon, too soon, the tropic storm
> Will out-blow the flick'ring lights
> Of human life-
> Our huts will fall
> In frailty upon the earth
> Whereon, they rot,
> And we, in foul disintegration
> Will be identified
> With dust.[31]

These four poets who are discussed briefly above are not the only poets who constitute the early phase of English-speaking West African poetry. Nnamdi Azikiwe, the first president of Nigeria, is part of this evolving tradition. His poetry has of late attracted critical attention, notably in a thorough-going appraisal of his ideo-aesthetic vision by Chukwuma Azuonye.[32] Thomas Dukar, Crispin George and Roland Dempster are also poets of Zik's and Armattoe's generation who have attracted critical attention, especially by writers like O.R. Dathorne.[33] In fact, to get a full range of the poetic output of the early elitist class and their nationalist aspirations and pretensions, we have to go back to Zik's collection, *Meditations*, where he lists "fellow verse-makers" he wishes to include in his intended anthology of African poetry. These poets, some of whom have published their collections of poetry since then, and some of whose poems have appeared occasionally in journals, newspaper and magazines include:

> Ade K. Agwu, Samuel B. Akpabot, Michael Dei-Anang, E.H. Appah, R.E.G. Armattoe, Bankole Awoonor-Renner Edwin T. Barclay, J. Benibengor Blay, J.B.Y. Borguaye, Roland T. Dempster, H.R.W. Diggs, Smart O. Ebbi, Jideofor Egbutcheh, Sam Ekpelle, C. Nelson Fyle, C.W. Gibson III, Gladys May Casley-Hayford, E. Ekeng Ita, Holman Jameson, Samuel Afolabi Johnson...[34]

Apart from these names, there are twenty other names listed in the same page who Zik felt were worthy of inclusion in his proposed anthology.[35]

The early West African poetry in English, loosely called "nationalist" poetry, is poetry of uncharted rebellion and improperly focused anger, and contains a hodge-podge of ideo-aesthetic visions that explain, as little else can, the character of the emergent elitist class. That the poetic compositions of these artists are artistically immature and stylistically mawkish are not even their fundamental deficiencies; it is their contradictory outlook, their class-imposed hesitations to combat imperialism, their romance with an abstract African past, their escapist ideo-political tendencies and appeal to universal human qualities that is essentially reducible to Western cultural irredentism that make their poetry weak and retrogressive when compared to the ideo-aesthetic pursuits of the poets of the 1970s and 1980s. It may not be historically correct to accuse them of being apologists of imperialism and reactionary liberal humanism, for we have to be objectively guided by the specificities of the social and cultural milieu that undergirded their art. Their poetic limitations and incapacities are organically related to and dialectically fused with the weakness of the elite as a vacillating, compromising and hesitating class. It is to this class that these poets belong and it is the ideology of this class that shaped their political and poetic direction, meaning for us that their poetic failure is a collective one – that of their class – and not the failure of any individual poet to realize his intended ideo-aesthetic vision.

Notes and References

1. Both Lewis Nkosi and Wole Soyinka have variously dismissed negritude as a pretentious poetic form or an escapist, narcissist and naïve celebration of a mythical, ahistorical African past.
2. Omafume Onoge, "Crisis of Consciousness in African Literature: A Survey" in G.M. Gugelberger, ed. *Marxism and African Literature* (London: James Curry Ltd, 1985), p. 23.
3. Ibid., p. 24.
4. In D.I. Nwoga, ed. *West African Verse* (London: Longman, 1967), p. 111.
5. Ibid., p. 110.
6. Aime Cesaire, *Return to my Native Land*, translated by John Berger and Anna Bostock, (London: Penguim Books, 1969), p. 75.
7. Ibid., p. 75.
8. Ibid., p. 75.
9. "Crisis of Consciousness" in *Marxism and African Literature*, pp. 26-27.
10. Ibid., p. 27.
11. *West African Verse*, p. 96.
12. *Marxism and African Literature*, p. 29.
13. Poems (1964), pp. 14-15.
14. O.R. Dathorne, *African Literature in the 20th Century* (London: Heinemann, 1974), 232.
15. See *Marxism and African Literature*, p. 29.
16. Ibid., p. 29.
17. *African Literature in the 20th Century*, p. 233.
18. *West African Verse*, p. 101.
19. See 'Introduction' to *The Wretched of the Earth* (Harmondsworth: Penguin, 1962), p. iv.

20. Lewis Nkosi's incisive criticism of Negritude appears in *Exile & Tradition* edited by Rowland Smith.
21. Eskia Mphahlele, an otherwise progressive critic, also subjected Negritude to scathing criticism. His observations are quoted in *Exile and Tradition*.
22. John Povey, a conservative Eurocentric critic equally lent a paternalistic voice on the debate over "Negritude". His assertion also appears in *Exile and Tradition*.
23. D.I. Nwoga who edited and introduced *West African Verse*, a collection of poems including the so-called Nationalist poetry, pointed out some of these deficiencies in the introduction of that collection.
24. *West African Verse*, pp. 15-16.
25. Ibid. p. 5.
26. Ibid., p. 7.
27. *African Literature in the 20th Century*, p. 154.
28. Raskhan, "The Poetry of Dr. R.E.G. Armattoe", *Presence Africaine*, no. 12 (Feb-March 1975), pp. 31-47.
29. *West African Verse*, p. 12.
30. "A Writer's Outlook", Ikyeame, 1 (July 1963), 40-43. Quoted in *African Literature in the 20th Century*, p. 168.
31. *West African Verse*, p. 21.
32. Ibid., p. 22.
33. In "The Poetry of Dr. Nnamdi Azikiwe", a seminar paper presented at the Centre for Igbo Studies of Abia State University, Uturu, Chukwuma Azuonye discusses Nnamdi Azikiwe's place as a poet, and delves into considerations of his thematic focus, stylistic devices and the limitations of his art.
34. In *African Literature in the 20th Century* (London: Heinemann, 1975), O.R. Dathorne discusses in detail the poetic craft of these "Nationalist" poets. He traces the origins of their poetry, their primary poetic concerns, the style of their art, and the artistic deficiencies of their works.
35. Nnamdi Azikiwe, *Meditations* (Nsukka: African Book Company, 1977), p. 25.

Part Three

ART AND IDEOLOGY IN POSTCOLONIAL AFRICAN POETRY: THE CRITICAL REALIST/RADICAL LIBERAL HUMANIST CONTEXT

Modern African poetry from the late 1950s to the early 1970s displays a plethora of creative visions and artistic searches; embodies a welter of contradictory sensibility and poetic consciousness on the vexing issue of the African experience; and elicits a large volume of critical responses comparable to those devoted to the fictional genre. It is of course expected that such a tradition of poetic activity, relatively unknown before in the continent, will generate profound attention and controversy, and excite the fertile imagination of readers, scholars and commentators. Retrospectively, we are placed in an advantageous position where we can take a sober critical look at the state of poetry in the immediate postcolonial period, mediate the acute contradictions inherent in the poetic creations of the time and periscope the efforts of the early critics and researchers in relation to emergent contemporary aesthetic attitudes and new creative media.

There is no doubt that modern African poetry of the period in question is a poetry of critical realism and radical liberal humanism, either in the realm of agitation for national political and socio-moral sanity, or in the front of resistance to the emasculation of African indigenous cultural values by a rampaging modernist sensibility. There is little doubt too, that the period witnessed one of the most amazing flowering of poetic talents, the display of varied and, oftentimes, contradictory perception of existing objective reality, and the agony of mental and physical torture of souls and minds caught in the asphyxiating circumstances of collective tragedies and national betrayal.

A lot of issues have been raised about the position of modern African poetry in relation to the emergence of national literary traditions, and some of them could be summarized thus: inward-gazing aesthetic imperative, when attention shifted from a fleeing colonial imperialism to offending black mismanagement;[1] the location of the problem posed by urbanization, capitalism and modernity as restricting and limiting influences on public poetic diction and mode of relevant communication;[2] the agony of speaking in a public voice when the protective cover of village communalism has collapsed, leaving only the remnants of shaky solidarity to confront an implacably entrenched privatist ethos;[3] the vociferously debated issue of obscurity (engendered by privatist idiom, inaccessible allusions, personal myth-making, uncrystallized foreign borrowings, linguistic incompetence, technical expertise, etc) and commitment (alertness to the ongoing historical and cultural transformation of Africa, awareness of the dilemma of neo-colonial globalism and the challenge posed by the crippling stupidity of an emergent African messenger class fulfilling the goals of imperialism);[4] the issue of domestication and Africanization; the paradox of traditionalist aesthetics remaining relevant in emergent industrial societies scalded deeply by several centuries of acculturating contacts; and the balance between functional traditionalist poetic modes and a somewhat socially irrelevant modernist poetic sensibility carried over from Europe.[5]

One way of looking at the significance of modern African poetry of this period, and one way of reviewing a small part of the existing literature in the field, is by taking a broad panoramic overview of the concern of most of the critics and scholars and the limitation of their scholarly efforts. This brief glance will afford us the opportunity of taking a closer snapshot of two or three of the notable poets of the period and underscore what actually constituted their main ideo-aesthetic direction.

Virtually all the commentators on the critical realist/liberal humanist poets of the 1960s were engaged in isolated, pocket-sized researches that produced sometimes brilliant flashes of insight and explicatory epiphany, which nevertheless leaves the overall picture smudged and blurred. By engaging in individual study of poets, as well as isolating them from their socio-historical habitat and denying them a coherent comparative exposure; and by stressing the production of several journal articles that cannot coherently articulate all the socio-aesthetic variables of the poems so studied, the scholars tended to produce numerous individual critical sketches. These limitations are not only applicable to journal articles and conference papers, but are discernible in more extended, book-length studies. Furthermore, most of these limitations are not manifest only in the critical efforts of the 1960s; they are similarly visible in the scholarly studies of the 1970s and even the 1980s and 1990s.

One major factor in favour of some of these critics, especially the pioneering scholars who wrote in the early and mid-1960s, and which can sufficiently be posited as the explanation for the vague generalizing nature of their criticism and the lack of in-depth historicity of their scholarship, is the very fact that they were charting a new course, and mapping the contours of a new terrain not previously traversed. Being pathfinders, they reposed the courage and boldness of resolute adventurers, and equally the crippling blindness of those searching for a hitherto unknown reality, especially when such is complex.

Being only aware of the wealth of English literature (American literature was still sufficiently marginalized in such schools as University College, Ghana; University College, Ibadan and Makerere University, Uganda in the 1940s and 1950s), and without the necessary intellectual and academic exposure to the forms and nature of African traditional art (African past, especially African spiritual and cultural past, of which literature is an integral part, is still seen by officially colonial, historical, sociological, anthropological and philosophical scholarship as an atavistic "one long night of savagery"). It is not surprising that they modelled their critical observations on the parameters evolved by English critics, and subscribed to critical criteria that suited the exploration of English literature. Nevertheless, the perceptive ones among them, and there are very many of them, went beyond the confines of their historical and ideological conditioning and the aesthetic limit-situations this set and enunciated some critical constructs that have been helpful to the critics of "Alternative Tradition" of the 1980s, to use Funso Aiyejina's pet term.

Virtually all the major aspects of literary discourse were handled by these critics, sometimes with soft sensitivity that is matchless and unsurpassed. They delved into the thematic structures of the poems, their imagistic, symbolic and ironic substances, their mythic and supra-historical essences, their linguistic embodiments, including narrative devices, and their general aesthetic and emotive features. In their study of the individual poets, they made attempt to place them squarely in their socio-historical environment, traced their poetic career and process of maturity, explicated the major influences in the works, and anatomized their basic concerns and their degree of success in handling such.

A contemporary study of modern African poetry, especially the poetry of the 1960s which was informed by critical realist sensibility and liberal humanist consciousness cannot dispense with the works of S. Anozie,[6] Paul Theroux,[7] Romanus Egudu,[8] Dan Izevbaye,[9] Donatus Nwoga,[10] G.

Heron,[11] Adrian Roscoe,[12] Bahadur Tejani,[13] Chinweizu *et al*,[14] Ali A. Mazrui,[15] O. R. Dathorne[16] and Chukwuma Azuonye.[17] These are among the most consistent and lucid commentators on the subject. Taken as a whole, their researches constitute the main highlights of the scholarship on these poets and their creative productions. Whatever their limitations may have been and these are glaring, their contribution to the development of modern African poetry is immense, their centrality in the overall context of evolving critical tradition in African literature is assured, just as it is impossible to come to any meaningful grips with the subject at hand without first perusing what they have left as legacy for us.

Having made these brief remarks about the nature of criticism of the first generation modern African poets, it is imperative that we turn our attention to the poets in question and see the basic relationship between art and ideology in their works.

It is fashionable for conventional scholarship to schematize the poetic outputs of various writers, classify them and codify them. This tendency to over-simplify the complex workings and patterns of socio-aesthetic articulations in these works result principally from the conscious attempt to fit the poets into narrow and parochial ideo-aesthetic models either inherited or created by the researchers. It is even more tempting for us now to do so, with the already mentioned advantage of looking at the poets from the position of near-complete knowledge of their creative career and productions. An example of this hasty attempt at over-generalization, schematization and crude codification is paraded by O.R. Dathorne in his *African Literature in the 20th Century*. In that study, Okigbo emerges as "the voice in ritual", Gabriel Okara's poetry is studied as being emblematic of "a disordered world", Ogbule Wonodo, as "the old man and life", Kofi Awoonor as essentially a "traditionalist", J.P. Clark as worthy of study simply because of his "technical ability", Kwesi Brew as engaging in "mock praise poem", Dennis Brutus as "lover and hater" and Okello Oculi's work as dealing solely with the "African as orphan,"[18] to mention a sizeable number of the poets he so categorizes.

It is not only Dathorne that is guilty of this simplistic schematization, but one or two examples from his work will make clear the gross limitation and critical inadequacy of that method, and help us to throw more light onto the essential artistic and ideological elements in the works of these poets. In his assessment of Chris Okigbo, Dathorne points out that:

> ... Okigbo transmutes all experience into ceremony.
> This process of transformation is the key to all Okigbo's verse:
> How can human beings grow again into gods, how can they regain their pristine state of spiritual innocence and yet retrain from their own sensuality?[19]

This statement could be forgiven if Dathorne were talking about "The Four Canzones" and the early sequences in *Heaven's gates* and *Limits*. But coming from a work which was published in 1975, three years after the publication of *Labyrinths*, the collection of Okigbo's poetry, which includes the "Path of Thunder" sequences, one is at a loss on what to say. Okigbo's development as a poet was a complex process which has been traced by many scholars, including Egudu, Anozie and Chinweizu et al. Surely, images and motifs of ritual passages, sacrifices and spiritual purgatory abound in his work, but to dismiss the creative effort of Africa's foremost poet as embodying only the thematic substance of a "voice in ritual" is to show a near-complete indifference to what Okigbo wrote. Themes as diverse as intellectual and artistic suppression and rebellion (a kind that reaches into revolutionary prophecy), abound in his work. Utilizing the vast resources of super-pository techniques, parallelism, catachresis, classical and Biblical allusions, repetitions, vernacular imagistic, metaphoric, symbolic and rhetoric narrative structures and forms of poetic articulations, and a somewhat convoluted privatist mythic idiom, Okigbo is able to synthesize the agony of the individual, the horror of alienation and exile, and the tragedy of a betrayed national ideal in his compact volume.

From the romantic exordium of "The Four Canzones" where his debt to the classists and the 20th century modernists was most manifest, and in which all the limitations pointed out by Chinweizu *et al* were so glaring, to the still privatist and obscure "Limits" and "Distances", the "poet's poet" found an oracular voice in the "Path of Thunder" sequences and ended his career as a "public servant".

It will be interesting to trace Okigbo's path of development and underscore how the complex medley of literary and supra-literary forces determined the new clear, now torturous path of an evolving artistic consciousness. Creative practice and the artistic individuality of the poet are dependent on socio-historical and socio-political forces and stimuli. The multiple articulations of over-determining material and non-material forces sometimes take the shape of contradictory perception of reality with all the complex episteme and vision that they produce and reproduce. In the case of Okigbo, we find a situation where a quiet though rebellious and daring soul honestly wishes to understand the variegated phases of reality – social and mythic – in an idiom borrowed from his wide readings. In this process, he reaches out to a tiny fragment of the emergent elitist literati, and demonstrates how that romantic vision could not stand the test of harsh historical reality.

First, the privatist images and obscure mythic structures of the Canzones (the 1950s) yielded, in the early 1960s to the snare of cultural awareness and nationalist sentiment (*Heaven's Gate*, especially the "Idoto" section and "Initiation"). This was because of the troubling effects of Western civilization with its spiritual appetizer – Christianity – and the tragic force of a rejuvenating traditionalist spiritual ethos beaten half-awake by the positive blows of nationalism. Secondly, we can detect the struggle between classical imagery and privatist thought with horrifying social and political tragedies in "Distances" and "Limits" as Nigeria passed from the euphoria of the "gathering of the tribes", in 1960 to the disputed census of 1963, the disputed general election of 1964 and the 1965 Western regional crisis.

Finally, in the "Path of Thunder" poems, there comes the resolution of Okigbo's turbulent search for identity, the inevitable victory of social concern over obscure personal delusions, and the high point of the marriage of art and life, aesthetics and politics. He achieved this through the oracular and prophetic declaration by a visionary who is conscious of his function as a voice of conscience.

The January 1966 coup, the May 1966 massacres in the North, the July 1966 counter-coup and the near decimation of the Igbo elite and masses that followed in its wake, all combined to make the process of producing these poetic sequences a reality. The social relevance of any true artist is also predicated on the historical crossroads of turbulent changes. His response to this turbulence, his participation in the debate of the day and his involvement in life's arguments – on the artistic and social fronts – are the genuine assurances of his greatness. Okigbo's greatness lies precisely in the fact of his being fully alive to his environment and its needs, his quick prophetic response to the agonies of existence, his ready attempt to popularize and democratize his art, and his fidelity to the common bonds of communal solidarity and "public prophecy" over a thinly-veiled quasi-modernist and pseudo-classical shamanism.

Like all the other critical realist/radical liberal humanist poets of the period who started by collaborating with the elitist nationalists (poems of cultural deracination and cultural nationalism) and ended up bitterly satirizing their misgovernance of society, Okigbo showed a remarkable degree of historical awareness of the fundamental principles of social change. His reactions to the socio-historical circumstances of the time were predicated on both the exigencies of his personal situation and his consciousness of the moral fiber of the moment. His art developed along the direction conditioned by the social concern of the period. The more he attempted to recoil into his privatist shell and the more convoluted and twisted the language, especially the syntax became, the more he was drawn, as though unwillingly, into the thick and thin, to use a trite but true adage, of political involvement, social engagement and moral clarification of social-historical tensions. The result of this is that at the end, he perfected his art by abandoning the exordious Canzones that recall lost worlds, the limits and distances of dark waters with their terrifying depths and scarred shores (scar of the crucifix of a kind) and embraced the pristine functions of his poetic ancestors: recounter, singer, drumbeater, rattler, prophet, seer, griot and moral guide. The development of his poetry from both the structural and thematic point of view, under the contexts of socio-historicity and ideo-aesthetics, will reveal the living soul of an elitist sympathizer of a neo-colonial establishment who realized, when it was nearly too late, that there is dignity and joy in critical realism and radical liberal humanism.

In commenting about the themes of the poetry of some West African poets, of which Okigbo is among, who are adjudged privatist, obscurantist and Euro-modernist, Romanus Egudu asserts:

> Personal psychological problems, the present African world of social immorality and political chaos, as well as the spectacle of human degeneration have ENGAGED the minds of West African poets. Thus in West African poetry the totality of man's environment – human, natural, and cosmic – is brought into play for the purpose of understanding the human situation in the context of both personal and universal experiences and projecting meaningfully into the future.[20]

It is, of course, clear that a brilliant but conservative critic like Romanus Egudu recognizes the imperative of socio-political concern as a determining factor of the aesthetic of modern West African poetry, and if we consider "Path of Thunder" we will readily discover that in no other poet of the period is this more manifest than in Okigbo, not even in Soyinka's political poems (*Idanre and other poems*, and *A Shuttle in the Crypt*) and J.P. Clark-Bedekeremo's "The Casualties".

It is interesting to note Egudu's concluding remarks about Okigbo and his poetry. Egudu argues that:

> .... Okigbo ranks highest among the four West African poets we have been studying. His consistent concern for the fate of the African indigenous (religious) culture in the face of Christianity in his earlier poems, and for the political upheavals in his country in his later poems, is evidence that he is deeply involved in the African predicament.[21]

Even though this otherwise powerful statement tells us little or nothing about the process of poetic growth and how Okigbo came to marry his art and ideology of social commitment, it still exposes something about the critical realist/liberal humanist conscience of the artist. Okigbo is surely one of the representative poets of the period and the one in whose work most of the ideals of critical realism and liberal humanism are manifest, as will be closely exemplified with "Path of Thunder" (poems prophesying war), the six sequences, as already mentioned, in which he broke the stranglehold of obscure Latinisms and far-flung distorted allusions to speak to his audience about the "magic" of the tragic times. It is, therefore, fitting that we end our comment on him by explicating one or two sequences in the lot.

In "Path of Thunder", Okigbo exposes his sharp and resolute concern for the fate of his countrymen groaning under a tottering but oppressive socio-political structure. In these sequences he brings out the deception of the political masters, the unchecked suppression of the common people and a prophetic vision of the eventual collapse of that horrendous order. To achieve this successfully, Okigbo applies the techniques of traditionalist aesthetic creative forms and narrative systems which Chinweizu et al identifies as "proverbs, dirges and elegies, praise names and praise songs, leader/choral antiphonies in traditional voice".[22] An example of these mode of oracular art expression is this:

> Condolences... from our swollen lips laden with condolence
> ... Thunder that has struck the elephant the same thunder can make a bruise Condolences.... Trunk of the iron tree we cry condolences when we break, shells of the open sea we cry condolences when we shake.[23]

Through this effective and refreshing use of natural images and symbols, and the repetition of the awe-inspiring CONDOLENCES, the critical realist and radical liberal humanist Okigbo, in articulating new ideological forms in his work, has powerfully brought out the wholesale battering of people and the inhuman decapitation of their essence, physical and spiritual. Equally, by adopting the tone of a communally-appointed town crier – denouncing, protesting, prophesying, informing and warning – he lays bare the organized barbarity that was Nigerian politics and state craft in the late sixties:

> The Robbers are here in black sudden steps
> Of showers, of caterpillars –
> The Eagles have come again
> The Eagles rain down on us –
> The politicians are back in giant hidden
> Steps of howitzers, of detonators...
> The Eagles descend on us,
> Bayonets and cannons ...[24]

The end of this section is remarkable, in its poignancy, immediacy and emotional appeal, and is worth reproducing:

> O Mother Earth, Unbind me
> Let this be my last testament: let this be
> The ram's hidden wish to the sword the
> Sword's secret prayer to the scabbard[25]

Okigbo's powerful critical vision, intense poetic insight and acute moral sensibility have transformed a basically topical and historical reality into the realm of the all-pervasive. This he does through the subtle and effective combination of political satire and caricature and enduring poetic devices, traditional and contemporary. Okigbo, of course, is a representative modern African poet of the immediate postcolonial period who attempted a blend of aesthetic ideal with social conscience and political involvement. Wole Soyinka is another such poet.

We have already pointed out that the 1960s was a period of acute contradictions in Africa. The apparent dichotomy between the emergent nation-states, subsisting on an amorphous nationalist consciousness acquired during the battle against colonial imperialism, and the dismantled colonial state apparatus has disappeared, to be replaced by the dichotomy engendered by socio-political and economic disequilibria wrought by the class structure of the postcolonial dispensation. Again, the homology of vision and close identification of objective suggestive of the actions of the literati and the political agitators in the 1950s have equally been replaced by bitter recrimination, vociferous dialogue, acrimonious exchanges and loss of belief. Affirmative consciousness, which inspired and sustained the ideo-aesthetic direction of the writings of the 1940s and 1950s turned, in the 1960s, to acute critical, inward gazing, publicist and propagandistic examination of the self-imposed social traumas and political tragedies and a resolute attempt to negate and defame the entire organized institutional structures of the emergent states.

Wole Soyinka is one writer who embodies most of the visible manifestations of inherent social contradictions germane to the postcolonial state apparatus. His writings as a whole, and not just his poetry, radically illustrate the consciousness of a caged spirit struggling for freedom; the image of the sensitive artist caught in the crossfire of past oddities and contemporary hallucinations; and the picture of self-imposed recluse, reclining on a quasi modernist and pseudo-traditionalist easy chair, shocked into active political engagement and social commitment by the force of circumstances beyond his personal control and direction.

From *A Dance of the Forests* to *Madmen and Specialists*; from *Idanre and other poems* to *A Shuttle in a Crypt*; and from *The Interpreters*, through *The Man Died* to *Season of Anomaly*,[26] the essential purpose, in fact the objective imperative of his art, is the shedding of the convoluted and largely mutilated idiom of a pretentious modernism and vain-glorious myth-making to the level of torturous commitment and public relevance, which yet bears the distorted scars of those wasted years of literary and artistic indirection. In capturing the morbid essence of a bloated "gathering of disparate 'tribes'", and in establishing the aesthetic and ideological framework for the de-romanticization and demystification of Africa in *A Dance of the Forest*, Wole Soyinka prepares the ground (still littered by obscurantist paradigms and untransformed mythic structures) for the condemnation of social cannibalism and institutionalized professional killings under the context of an existing social milieu in *Madmen and Specialists*. In his poetry which concerns us here, we note the gradual uncloaking of the suffocating garb of a complex and confused Ogun hacking his way through the ranks of friends and foes and shockingly enjoying his dual status as creator and destroyer, to the donning of the mantle of critical realism and social satire in "October, 66", "Flowers for My hand", and which reaches a high water mark in the celebratory sequences in *A Shuttle in a Crypt*.

Despite Soyinka's weaknesses, and they are many; one, as a consciously creative individual with substantial inadequacies of artistic vision and creative insight and, two, as a member of a class, the elitist class of radical liberal humanists, with all the stamps of liberalism; and despite the self-inflicted weaknesses which are products of his deliberate allegiance to obscurantist modernism and cultic mythic idioms (convoluted imagery, syntactic obfuscation and other types of linguistic irascibility), his later poetry reflect a conscious awareness of his immediate environment and his attempt to interpret experience on the agenda generated and conditioned by the socio-political circumstances of the time.

In making this assertion, we will look briefly at one poem from *A Shuttle in a Crypt* in order to substantiate our reading of Soyinka as a critical realist and radical liberal humanist. In *A Shuttle in a Crypt* (poems from prison), he demonstrates a remarkable grasp of the oppressive culture of silence and fear that has gripped the Nigerian nation, on a general level, and the prison inmates on a specific level. In the poem, "Procession: Hanging Day", he recounts the death of five political detainees because the sounds of their footsteps he has been hearing for three days are no longer heard.

This harrowing political murder is brought out in the poem through three successive stages or movements. The first movement is highly descriptive and contains his attempt to capture the reality of the doomed prisoners:

> Echoes footsteps of the grave
> Procession glances that would
> Conjure up a draw bridge...
> Tread. Drop. Tread. Drop. Dead

The second movement incarnates potent images of tragedy and hopelessness through the deployment of highly revealing rhetorical questions:

> What may I tell you? What reveal? Who before them
> peered unseen? Who stood one-legged on the
> untrodden verge – lest I should not return. What I
> tell you of rigorous of the law? What whispers to

their football thunders Vanishing to shrouds of
sunlight?

This comment moves to the level of condemnation of the
entire structure of oppression and injustice disguised as
justice:

> Let no man speak of justice, guilt
> Far away, blood-stained in their tens of
> Thousands... hands that damned
> These wretches to the pit triumph
> But here, alone the solitary deed.

Through the use of poetic devices such as the metaphor "the wall of prayer", meaning the wall dividing the section where the prisoners pray and sing, the image, "conjure up a drawbridge", that describes the frightened look of the detainees who tended to stare vacantly, and the hyperbolic "their football thunder", suggesting the heavy sounds of the boots worn by the police and wardens, Soyinka recreates an agonizing picture of hopelessness, captivity and human degradation.

Abiola Irele's observation that Soyinka's concern with an individual view of the world amounts to "an almost exclusively personal awareness of things, of events and of peoples"[27] and Uli Beier's argument that in his later poetry, Soyinka has shown concern for "more serious, more difficult subjects, and his language has become far richer in imagery"[28] are among the earliest critical commentaries on Soyinka's poetry, and may have contributed in helping to foist the tag of obscurity on the poet who might have been influenced by what Chinweizu *et al* would adjudge as Euro-modernist and Eurocentric critical sensibility. By mystifying an already obfuscated world, struggling between the jingles of the iron bells of mythic structures and the resounding clangs of social upheavals, these early critics cemented Soyinka's marriage with the first tendency, thereby limiting the scope of his art and his audience and, in that process, denying himself the opportunity of becoming a great African poet, which surely he ought to be.

This celebration of an undefined individualism and iconoclasm (the one that borders on social nihilism and psychic alienation) in Soyinka's poetry is equally noticeable in O.R. Dathorne's supposed eulogization of Soyinka's lack of commitment. He encapsulates his view of Soyinka thus:

> Wole Soyinka's poetry, some of which is collected in Idanre (1967), marks a progression of intellectual growth – from the alienated individual who satirizes society to the protagonist who has attained a new understanding of what his culture means....
>
> He is far more sensitive to the causality of inner hurt that has resulted from his being linked to contrary cultures, and this accounts for the quiet reflective mood of his poetry. After the public-speaking tone of some of his contemporaries, Soyinka's privacy is a fitting corrective.[29]

A fitting corrective to what? one may ask. Of the public concern of his contemporaries? Of their mistake in analyzing the socio-political tensions and traumas of their society in accessible language and clear imagery? Of rising above the claptrap of a vacuous individualism and elitist alienation that seem to be the only measure of intellectuality and exulted artistic individuality?

One wonders whether it is the same Wole Soyinka who experimented with a pseudo-Marxist ideology in the early 1960s; who was accused of holding up a radio station and substituting a regional premier's prepared speech with his own; who spoke sharply against the near genocidal action of the Gowon government and earned for himself a solitary confinement for his labour; who, even in prison, kept on reflecting about social existence (producing *A Shuttle in a Crypt* and *The Man Died*) as a gesture to that reflection and what it means for his people; and who was self-exiled in the 1990s battling against inhuman odds for the restoration of democracy and accountable government in Nigeria that Dathorne is writing about. Surely, some of the issues observed by Dathorne are to be found in Soyinka's poetry, but to suppress the social content of his work, to destroy his ideological loyalty to radical liberal humanism and to alienate him from the society whence he emerged and which conditions his perceptions and artistic vision, by reading his work as purely shamanistic and narcissistic pieces is, to say the least, a gross error in critical judgement and a poor understanding of the complex nature of art, especially in its relation to objective reality.

When we come to the poetry of Okot P'Bitek, we inevitably arrive at a problematic juncture because of Bitek's dual position as a cultural reviver and positive nationalist and a conservative traditionalist hankering after lost ideals in a romantic fashion that echoes Senghor's mystical Negritude. On the one hand, we find the celebrant of the communal ethos of a forgotten past, and, on the other hand, a sharp critical realist satirizing the evils of postcolonial governance and capitulation to Western values and precepts. Where do we begin to study the man? How do we approach a figure so venerated that any attempt to criticize him is sure to generate rancorous replies and vociferous meta-criticisms. The point of departure is to appreciate the effusive welcome that greeted the arrival of "Song of Lawino".

Adrian Roscoe observes thus in *Uhuru's Fire*:

> His (Bitek's) career has been a model of what negritude apostles preached but did not always practice. He first achieved fame with an English version of Song of Lawino a poem so immediately successful that it became at once the chosen model for a whole school of writing. Okello Oculi wrote his Orphan in frank limitation of it: Joseph Buruga's The Abandoned Hut is in the same form, and Okot himself has followed Lawino with Song of Ocol, Song of Malaya, and Song of a Prisoner.[30]

From Ngugi wa Thiong'o:

> "Song of Lawino" is the one poem that has mapped out new areas and new directions in East African poetry. It belongs to the soil. It is authentically East African in its tone and in its appeal. This can be seen in its reception: it is read everywhere, arousing heated debates.[31]

From Okello Oculi:

> "Song of Lawino" touched exactly that nerve which we had been arguing. The response of Kampala was so spontaneous ... he (Okot) confirmed this yearning we had for self-assertion, not only in terms of ourselves, but in the collective sense, what we felt was the African sense of assertion.[32]

Some of these unrestrained encomiums are pardonable judging the historical circumstances that produced them. The euphoria generated by the production of good and worthy creative works had not died down in the 60s, thus most scholars and writers felt justifiably elated when some great work is added to the growing stable of genuinely patriotic works challenging white supremacy, the erosion of cultural values and the pathetic imitativeness of the elite who are truly "white skin, black mask". The initial reception of "Song of Lawino" is subjectively predicated on its being looked at as a work of cultural affirmation, as being an upholder of authentic indigenous values harassed by capitalism, and its handmaiden, Christianity. Its initial appeal is also based on the imperative engendered by the over-simplification of the contradictions it supports and negates: the past is wholesome, the present is atavistic, and African values are positive values, western values are negative values. This over-simplification of a stereotypical situation that is grossly distorted and misunderstood also generates the euphoric response by Afrocentric scholars who accepted unquestioningly the hidden socio-cultural imperatives of the work and adopted the poet's ideo-aesthetic position without subjecting same to critical materialist reading.

A retrospective reading of "Song of Lawino" and "Song of Ocol", from a materialist position, shows the emptiness of both Lawino's and Ocol's positions, their false exaggerations and highly inadequate understanding of the dialectics of social change, especially in the area of the qualitative succession of social formations. Lawino's call for an unbridled African past unaffected by the trammeling forces of culture contact and dynamic inter-racial and international associations (thus denying that reality the benefit of the gains made by other civilizations) is as hollow as Ocol's total alienation from his African roots, his loss of organic social intercourse with his people and environment, his brazen adoption of undiluted Western civilization and his apish disposition which lacks coherence.

Lawino's traditional world is a static world, a world where history has virtually stopped, a world that denies the logic of inherent social change as an integral part of the dynamics of social renewal. Ocol's is a world of alienation and social rootlessness, a world where something strange and alien has been imposed. These two extreme polarities of vision in the two collections seem to us to lie at the base of the first phase of Bitek's art. The ideo-aesthetic structure of his art at this juncture could be summarized as a romantic and idealistic apprehension of African past in the "mystic affirmative consciousness"[33] tradition of Senghor and a lack of objective understanding of the process of historical development and the necessary, and sometimes, inevitable corruption of socio-cultural and socio-political structures which cannot exist immanently and immutably.

We can isolate two major tendencies in Bitek's art: the tendency which we have already mentioned in the preceding paragraph and the tendency which evolved in his later art. This later tendency is his critical examination of the nature and content of politics and social organization and institutions in postcolonial African setting. Actually, this tendency had started to emerge in "Song of Lawino", in the section "The Buffaloes of Poverty Knock the People Down." This is where Okot abandons his near-narcissistic admiration of the African past and turns his attention on the burning issues of the day in the manner that does not reek of the over-simplified Africa-Europe dichotomy. In fact, the content of that section is a remarkable manifestation of Bitek's deep concern about the fate of his country and people. This critical realist/radical liberal humanist tendency that poked its head in Song of Lawino emerges forcefully and becomes stabilized as a mature ideo-aesthetic vision in "Song of Malaya" and "Song of Prisoner". It is through a brief look at that relevant section of "Song of Lawino" and an equally brief glance at "Song of Prisoner" and "Song of Malaya" that we intend to justify our inclusion of Okot P'Bitek as a poet whose ideo-aesthetic vision is informed by critical realism/radical liberal humanism.

Song of Lawino contains, as part of its minor thematic thrust, but in essence a much more important issue of contemporary socio-political relevance than the over-rated major theme, elements of sad political commentary on the drift and anarchy that set in with 'flag independence' in many African countries. Through the contrasting of two rival political "factions" – whose guiding ideologies are ill-defined and vaguely articulated – Lawino is able to puncture their call for freedom, peace and unity and their utter disregard for the yearning of the masses:

> With the coming
> Of the new political parties
> My husband roams the country-
> side like a wild goat...

He engages in empty pontificating and perpetuates the disharmony between him and his brother. She captures the tendency succinctly:

> Ocol does not enter his brother's house
> You would think
> There was homicide between them...

This cosmetic quarrel, lacking substantial ideological content, is symbolic of the wider intra-elite political bitterness and acrimony that have been imposed on the country by the emergent class of black leaders.

Lawino further uses imagistic patterns of symbolic implicatur to signify the neglect of the poor, their sufferings and woes, while the new leaders, including her husband and her husband's brother, engage in futile and energy-sapping mock combats:

> And while the pythons of sickness
> Swallow the children
> And the buffaloes of poverty
> Knock the people down
> And ignorance stands there
> Like an elephant,
> The war leaders
> Are tightly locked in bloody feuds
> Eating each other's liver...

Thus, by utilizing the multi-faceted and multifarious resources of oratory, especially lament and dirge, rhetorical question (why do they split up the army into two hostile groups?), graphic imagery (the politicians are like the python/with a bull water buck in its tummy), and appeal (where is the peace of Uhuru? Where is the unity of independence?), Okot drives home his critical commentary and elevates a basically situational problem to the height of the enduring and recurring.

In Song of Prisoner, Okot, through the narrator, recreates an imaginative agony of a political detainee incarcerated because of his murder of a political leader, who Okot has revealed to be Tom Mboya,[34] through the persuasion and influence of an opportunistic political careerist who is "now warming the prisoner's bed with his wife" and commiting other despicable atrocities. Okot cleverly projects, through the image of the suffering detainee's yearning for freedom, his criticism of the complacent ideology and anti-people policies of the political leadership. He assails the foibles of a newly independent nation with all the pious talks of freedom by her rulers, talks which end up being actualized as the suppression of the masses, political murders and imprisonment of opponents and social critics.

For example, in the thirteenth segment of the poem, the prisoner, through the now familiar and consistent style of lament, evocative and incantatory sequences, appeal, imagistic patterns, symbolic structures and rhetorical questions, feels the loss of freedom acutely as he remembers the funeral anniversary of his father's death:

> Is today not my father's
> Funeral anniversary
> My clansmen and clanswomen
> Are gathering in our village,
> They sit in circles
> In the shades of granaries
> But who will make
> The welcome speech?

He expresses his nostalgia in these imagistic patterns:

> Men drink kwete beer
> Women cook goat meat
> And make millet bread
> But I am not there...

He also draws our sympathy forcefully to his utter depression which easily compels us to condemn his gaolers. When he could no longer bear the torment in his mind and the fever-pitch degree of his imagination, he burst out into a frantic and defiant chant:

> I want to join
> The funeral dancers
> I want to thread the earth

> With a vengeance
> And shake the bones
> Of my father in this grave!

Apart from the bitter social criticism one finds in "Song of a Prisoner", we also have ready example of Okot's caustic satire of the debased state of morality, sexual abuse and spiritual decay in "Song of Malaya", a collection which exposes the depravity, cunning and cleverness of an unrepentant prostitute. Through her declarations and testimonies – a sort of confessional statement – she exposes the whole range of lawyers, doctors, teachers, politicians, bankers, and even clergymen who patronize her. In accusing a clergyman of lack of virility, she charges:

> Your silly baby tortoise
> Withdraw its shrunken skinny neck...
> Leaving me on fire
> The whole night long

On another occasion, the prostitute accuses a teacher of contributing to general moral atrophy and spiritual sterility of the society because of his corrupt sexuality. Instead of teaching his students morally edifying subjects, he uses them as experimental guinea pigs to test his sexual prowess:

> How many teenagers
> Have you clubbed
> With your large-headed hammer,
> Sowing death in their
> Innocent fields?

Okot P'Bitek is surely one of Africa's most vibrant poets. Though his cultural aggression is idealistic and somewhat misdirected, his healthy dose of social satire on the state of society marks him out as a sensitive artist alive to his social responsibilities. It is, therefore, rewarding to note the increasing attention paid his work by scholars. In a 1975 summary of his writings, especially on the issue of political satire and critical realism which is central to our discussion,

O.R. Dathorne says:

> Neither "Song of Lawino" nor "Song of Ocol" states the case as bitterly as this poem (Song of Prisoner) does. One might say that whereas the first two poems mask ... the issue of lack of concern, Song of Prisoner openly and forcefully reveals its reality. Recurrent images of lost virility have more impact here for the protagonist is concerned not just with his lack of social grace but with the complete emptiness of all he professes to be.[35]

Though this statement is inadequate as a summary of Okot's critical social vision and his commitment to humanity, one can say that it is a good start for a proper socio-historical and ideo-aesthetic contextualization of Okot P'Bitek's art. From G.A. Heron's *The Poetry of Okot P'Bitek*,[36] which is substantially flawed as all books with chapter concepts representing different texts and not ideas are bound to be, and which too owes allegiance to the summary-commentary style of criticism, to Egudu's highly incisive and controversial article, "Society as Victim of the individual – P'Bitek's Song of Malaya",[37] a lot of critics and scholars have started responding to the creative productions of one of Africa's finest poets. It is worthy, in this regard, to mention the efforts of A. Ejughemre,[38] M. Ruchoya,[39] M. Folarin,[40] Ogo Ofuani,[41] Bahadur Tejani,[42] G. Heron,[43] Maina Gathungu,[44] Ngugi Wa Thiong'o,[45] S.O. Asein,[46] Reed Chapelle,[47] A. Heywood,[48] M. Margaret,[49] R. Serumaga[50] and Michael Ward.[51] Of course, no account of the scholarship on Okot P'Bitek can be complete without a mention of the contribution of Adrian Roscoe. Roscoe's extensive discussion of the poetry of Okot under the title, "Okot P'Bitek and the Song School" in his *Uhuru's Fire*,[52] is one of the most sustained studies of his work and the one which attempts to place him squarely in the context of Africa's literary and social development. The study also underscores Okot's position as a literary artist and a cultural activist and analyzes his influence on other poets of East Africa and elsewhere.[53]

We cannot conclude our discussion on critical realist/radical liberal humanist African poets, especially of the first ten postcolonial years, without mentioning the work of Jared Angira. Angira occupies a special position in the overall context of African poetry, particularly as regards his inclusion as a poet of the postcolonial period as the substantial part of his work was written in the 1970s while the other poets we have been considering wrote in the 60s. That Angira is a second-generation poet is obvious, but that most of his poems appeared in journals in the late 1960s (4 or 5 years after Kenyan independence) is also an established fact. His first collection of poems, *Juices,* was published in 1970, 7 years after Kenya won her independence and between 4-10 years when the bulk of African countries gained their independence. Furthermore, Angira's poetry is suffused with the same spirit of critical realism and militant liberal humanism that characterize the works of the other poets we have been discussing. It is, therefore, because of the nearness of his initial writing to the period we are analyzing and his ideo-aesthetic affinity with the first generation poets that warrant his inclusion in this section.

Jared Angira is, without doubt, a fine poet. Within a short period after the publication of *Juices,* he has attracted wide-ranging critical attention, which unequivocally establishes the solidity of his vision, the complexity of his artistry, the appropriateness of his techniques and his unquestionable commitment to the cause of social amelioration through a satiric mode that denigrates the oddities of existence – especially oppression and exploitation. With over five collections to his credit (*Juices*, 1970; *Silent Voices,* 1972; *Soft Corals,* 1973; *Cascades,* 1979; and *The Year Go By,* 1980) his place as one of African's most vibrant and enterprising poets is already assured.

Chris Nwanjala sees him as the best gifted poet in East Africa while Angus Calder feels that even as an author without a collection of poems, he possesses several poetic styles and techniques[54] and affirms in a different paper that as a poet, Angira "is an alert, witty writer, capable of cleverly masked detachment, of conveying simultaneously a strong emotion and a critique of it."[55] Adrian Roscoe, on his own, discovers in his poetry "good clear imagery, a gift for compression, amphoric echoes of tradition, moral concern and verbal coinages which combine to produce highly effective verse"[56] while Abdul Yesufu points out that Angira's poetry is socially relevant because it is:

> Clearly focused on a living social reality, presenting various facets of this reality, especially the social lapses and the results of these defects on the overall social order. In his depiction of his society the poet sympathetically handles themes and ideas expose and comment on such ills as economic disparity, social and political corruption, sexual immorality, de-culturization and the paradox of political independence.[57]

All these critical observations are in line with Bahadur Tejani's assessment that Angira's poetry has "a delicacy of language and organization and poetic prize that is matchless,"[58] and Timothy Wangusa's assertion that:

> Angira's poetry is full of energy and movement; it is full of violent action: ploughing, cascading, swimming, ferrying across, flying, rolling, beating against rock.[59]

All these critical observations are important in placing Angira in the context of modern African poetry and establishing his links with the tradition of artistic sensitivity and social vision that underscore committed African writing. These critical opinions, nevertheless, do not and cannot smooth over the defects of Angira's art, the least not being the sometimes apologetic tone of some of his works, the hesitations in others and his inability to harness his enormous poetic skill towards the task of positing a clear socio-political direction for the broad mass of the people. These failings will be looked at closely later. Before that, however, we will substantiate our claim about Angira's critical realism and liberal humanism by looking at two or three of his poems from the collection, *Juices*.

Angira wrote in the preface to *Juices*:

> There I learnt that each hour has its truth, that you cannot squeeze out of man more than is in his resource... Now each time I stand before the red Carpeted dais listening to some upgraded being of the upward order tell us to be quiet... Sam Butler waves up his Hu'dibra and shouts between my thighs: he that complies against his will is of his own opinion still ... I am waiting for the power cut-cum-eclipse then I will raid humanity's plantation.[60]

Being not ready to comply "against his will" and thereby "remain still", Angira wrote highly incisive poems that satirize vehemently the oppression in his society. Dedicated to the common man, *Juices* touches on such topics as political brutality and legal justice, the belief in the future triumph of an undefined and vaguely articulated, but nevertheless, positive popular ideal, and sarcastic comments on the relics of the politically oppressive and economically exploitative colonial past.

"The Final Judgment," one of the poems in the collection, is an irreverent attack on the nature of judgement under an oppressive socio-political and judiciary system. A man rightly avenges the murder of his brother, only to be hanged in the gallows for "taking the law into his own hands". But the poem transcends the political and social planes and reaches out to the metaphysical when the judges are tried by God for their inhuman justice while God himself awaits his own judgment, for the circle to be completed.

The poem is based on a dialectical unity which shows the confusion that is the lot of man in his attempt to understand his political and social environment. One problematic action begets another that seems to have no definite solution:

> .... Made him murder his brother's killer
> ... Who judged him fit
> For nothing but the gallows
> And God judged them fit
> For nothing but hell
> When God shall stand
> Before a great wise jury
> And be judged for helping many...

This dialectical arrangement is an expression of the poet's awareness of the futility of political repression couched in legal terms because that repression, instead of solving the imagined problem or quelling the inevitable trouble, imposes other traumas that return to possess and torment the perpetrators.

The use of the repetitive refrains: "It was an eye for an eye and it was a tooth for a tooth", is not only allusive to the Mosaic legal system that existed when such laws were made; it also should be pointed out that the "gallowed" man is symbolic of all the dispossessed while 'the uniformed" and "grey-haired judges" symbolize the coercive and repressive arm of the subjugating political class.

In "In One Pot", Angira returns to the theme of political rivalry and betrayal of the goals of Uhuru, already mentioned in connection with Okot P'Bitek. The emergent black leaders' interest is the capture and control of state power and nothing more. In their frenzied bid for domination and leadership, they alienate a large chunk of the citizenry, quarrel with their political opponents who belong to hostile parties and end up emphasizing the divisiveness associated with "each cock crowing in its own village".

Angira uses mostly natural and agricultural imagery and terms to suggest the rural and peasant background of the emergent new rulers – thereby sharply exposing their artificial sophistication. These images also highlight the political factions clamouring for leadership and dominance:

> From the reeds
> From the hills
> From where potatoes thrive
> From where carvers crowd
> From where the palm trees sing...

Drawing on the desecration of the old adage that there cannot be two captains in one ship (here it assumes an animal symbolic imagery suggestive of death: "two cocks never cook in one pot"), the poet pinpoints the disarray, confusion and incessant upheavals and instability that have been the lot of postcolonial African states. The inability of the politicians to prove false that adage ("it shall be proven false"); their dispersal into their little kingdoms ("each cock crows in its village gate"), and the effectiveness of the animal and natural images and symbols are indicative of Angira's belief in the capacity of the common man to understand his world and struggle to change it. This idea is taken up in such poems as "Rape I" and "Dry Tears" which contain very biting political statements. In them, he deals with the question of social consciousness and liberty by projecting the political leaders as bad and incompetent and making the masses capable of seeing through them:

> Every day they have acted
> And left the stage
> But only parrots
> Have learnt their morals.

In his later collections, Angira broadens his social vision, extends the scope of his satire and social criticism and becomes more relentless in his condemnation of the ugliness of social existence in a society defined by the spirit of necrophilia. It is not only politics, but also prostitution and other forms of sexual abuse and perversion, poverty, (or more appropriately, destitution) and other forms of social deprivation that are the dominant socio-aesthetic elements in his poetry. It is expected that with this broadening of vision, critics will devote more time to his poetry in order to clearly bring to the fore his artistic experimentation and social commentary.

The four poets discussed briefly here are by no means the only critical realist poets of the period under survey. Nevertheless, they are representative. The first three illustrate the critical tendencies of the early and mid-1960s, while the last is indicative of the probing liberal humanism of the late 1960s and early 1970s. Poets like Taban Lo Liyong (*Another Nigger Dead* and *Franz Fanon's Uneven Ribs*), Lenrie Peters (Satellites) and J.P. Clark-Bedekeremo (*Casualties and Other Poems*) are very central to the tradition we are talking about. Their works have received serious attention in book-length studies, journal articles, research papers, seminar and conference papers and theses and dissertations. Dathorne's *African Literature in the 20th Century*; A. Roscoe's *Mother is Gold* and Uhuru's *Fire*; Chinweizu et al's *Toward the Decolonization of African Literature* and Kofi Awoonor's *The Breast of the Earth* are few of the numerous works dealing with the poetry of the above-mentioned and others not mentioned. Recently too, young, dynamic and increasingly radical scholars are beginning to bring their critical searchlight to bear on the poetry of some of these long established poets. An example of this critical rejuvenation is Ezenwa-Ohaeto's revolutionary aesthetic reading of the poetry of Taban Lo Liyong.[61]

J.P. Clark is another poet who deserves brief mention in this sum up. He is very much concerned about the state of the Nigerian polity in the mid 1960s, and like the other critical realist poets of the period, turned his attention to the aesthetic mediation of the tragedy of that historical moment and the agony of existence in an atrophied and doomed environment. *His Season of Omens*[62] is very much about the politics of Nigeria's First Republic and is prophetic about the impending collapse and annihilation of that dispensation. In R.N. Egudu's words:

> J.P. Clark sees the politics of that era in Nigeria as an

exercise in hypocrisy and dishonesty. To him it was a period "when ministers legislated from bed and/ made high office the prize (reward) for failure "; when wads of notes were kept in infant skulls/with full blessing of prelates"; when women grew heavy with ballot papers delivering/the entire house to adulterers"; and "when the grand vizier in season of arson turned/upon bandits in a far off place', and that is, pretending not to notice worse bandits – the agents of arson – at home.[63]

This kind of politics readily prepares the ground for popular discontent, general disillusionment and universal loss of hope about the relevance of leadership and governance. Inevitably, attempt will be made to overhaul the moribund system. It is the Five Majors, referred to in the poem as the "five hunters", who undertake this task of socio-political purification of the society, leaving in their wake carnage and revolutionary disorder, with most leaders of the political order dead. As the poet puts it:

> One morning
> The people woke up to a great smoke
> There was fire all night,
> But who lighted it, where
> The lighter of the fire
>
> Fallen in the grass was the lion,
> Fallen in the forest was the jackal
> Missing by the sea was the shepherd sheep

Egudu's concluding remark in his analysis of the poem can readily serve our own summing up interest here. Egudu says:

> Though poetry is not history, this poem has presented us with fresh interpretations of such political features as election, political appointments, political governance, and coup, which (interpretations) help us appreciate those events more deeply than ever before.[64]

It is even in the poem "The Casualties", the culmination of Clark's poetic vision on the Nigerian crisis, especially the civil war, that his gift as a poetic stylist and user of ironic and paradoxical structures of signification come to light. The poem that dispenses with the everyday understanding of what war casualties are, and leads probingly to an apprehension of those he considers the real casualties, who ordinarily we would be reluctant to give that miserable tag. It is not that Clark refuses to see the tragedy of the war in terms of the agonies of the physical and emotional sufferers of the war carnage; he gives ample space to them and their woes, but he seems to hurry over them, to foreground them and then dismiss them in order to be able to present for us the categories of people he considers the most tragic casualties of the war.

Clark starts by telling us that the casualties "are not only those who are dead", for in a way even, "they are well out of it", neither are they "only those who are wounded, nor only those who have lost persons or property". The list also includes, "those who are led away by night", and "those who started a fire and now cannot put it out" and those who, "escaping the shattered homes shall become prisoners in/A fortress of falling walls". Having dispensed with the list of people readily and naturally looked upon as war casualties he moves to those occult zones of poetic insight and inspiration to discover for himself and humanity the real, but concealed casualties of the war. These are:

> .. The emissaries of rift,
> So smug in smoke-rooms they haunt abroad
> At home eating up the forests
> They are the wandering minstrels who, beating on...
> Into a dance with rites it does not know

For Clark, therefore, the most pitiable casualties of the war are ambassadors, government agents and creative writers, involved in the war because, unlike the maimed, the jailed and the 'propertyless', they can never conceive of themselves as being casualties in their comfort and physical health. It is by referring to these categories of people as casualties; by denigrating their official position and political role; by casting a half-mocking, half-ironic, half-critical and half-sympathetic and pitying eye at them that the poet achieves his intent. This is also a means through which the poem derives its power. Clark, the critical realist, demonstrates his knowledge (consciously held and intuitively grasped) of the ideo-aesthetic properties of radical liberal humanism nowhere better than in "The Casualties." On the surface, one can even accuse Clark of aesthetic and moral distantiation and odious fence-sitting, but a deep look at his position will reveal a level of political commitment which is as dangerous as that of those on the two mutually opposed and irreconcilable sides. In the poetically horrifying picture he paints of an anarchical political and social situation, by measure of this distantiation and aloofness, he fails to realize that his apparent non-involvement is dangerous involvement in the conflict. The unconscious significance of the poem therefore lies on the idea of the poet as one of the CASUALTIES, one of those psychically and spiritually mangled by the war, just as the "emissaries and the minstrels" are.

Lenrie Peters' "In the Beginning"[65] and Crispin Hauli's "The Song of the Common Man"[66] are two ready examples of the subject matter of critical realist poetry. Peters is an established African poet who has already been mentioned in passing. Crispin Hauli is a Tanzanian poet whose vision of the horror of living of the poor finds ready poetic expression in the poem under discussion and several others written in the mid and late 1960s and collected in several anthologies.

In "In the Beginning" – a counter-positional exchange between an impoverished peasant and a wealthy and influential politician, we see the whole range of social and material deprivations that are the lot of the peasant: hunger, illiteracy destitution and want. The inquisitiveness of the peasant to know when all these thing will be provided for him leads to his incarceration because, such potentially hot-headed elements, as far as the politician is concerned, are the repository of revolutionary thoughts and the lighters of the fire of social upheaval. The poem, just as some other poems in Peter's collection, *Satellites*, make cogent statements about institutionalized inequality, moral debasement and general spiritual decay of society and help in placing him as one of Africa's critical realist/liberal humanist poets worthy of closer attention and more detailed study.

What more can we add about the poetry of these critical realist poets? It is true that literary works have a near inexhaustible potential, in idea-content and style, and are capable of responding to different approaches of criticism, under different contexts, without yielding all their meaning. It is precisely this inexhaustible potential that the "new critics" (formalists, essentially) have in mind when they chose as the motto of their journal, the expression, "the last verse has not yet been sufficiently explicated". It is, therefore, necessary to point out that the poets we have been dealing with and the movement they all belong to will continue to elicit controversial literary debates, an example being the Chinweizu et al versus Soyinka diatribe on traditionalist aesthetics, Neo-Tarzanism, Euro-modernism, Euro-criticism, and all the other vexing issues relating to commitment, obscurity and the domestication of modern African poetry. Even D.I. Nwoga's systemization of the main variables of this argument in his "Modern African Poetry: The Domestication of a Tradition" seems not to have laid to rest significant gaps and omissions in this dynamic aesthetic field; if anything it has opened up one or two other areas of argument.

This is but one side of the complex, multi-faceted aspects of the problem of articulating the full range of the socio-aesthetic and socio-historical imperatives of critical realist poetry in Africa. A lot of works have, nevertheless, been done by serious scholars, and we have tried to list, as much as possible, some of the major works in the area as a guide to discerning readers. Some of the researches in the field are, however, highly pretentious, opportunistic and insincere as the attempt is to redefine modern African poetry in the context of a non-existing tradition and force foreign aesthetic imperatives on the emergent poets. The end result of this is that scholarly works are produced that lack organic interconnection and link with the actual experimentation in the creative field; works which fail to understand the complex nature of critical realism, note its transitional nature and underscore its qualitative transformation into a higher, revolutionary art.

Critical realism is a transitory phase in the growth of any national and, to a considerable extent, continental literature. Its main features include a sharp vituperative criticism of a comprehensively depicted reality; the individualistic tone and content of the creative work; the somewhat static nature of the reality depicted; the irresolution noticeable in the handling of the conflict; and its now gradual, now fast-paced transformation into revolutionary art.[67] These features are as cogent for African critical realist poetry as they are for African prose-fiction and drama. African poetry, especially that of the 1960s and early 1970s, is hampered and deformed by some of the above-noted tendencies of that ideo-aesthetic method, including the vexing question of privatist and obscurantist myth-making, uncontrolled elliptical and allusive quality of the poetic references, imitativeness, and the apparent divorce between the artist (pretending to be alienated) and his community. Some of these handicaps and limitations have been overcome by a few of the poets; Okigbo, for example, in "Path of Thunder", as noted by Chinnweizu et al. As a transitional phenomenon, critical realism and radical liberal humanism inevitably give way to a revolutionary socio-aesthetic form in modern African poetry, an aesthetic of the late 1970s, 1980s and 1990s whose highly assertive, combative and partisan nature is a reflection of the heightened political, economic and cultural contradictions and dislocations in very many postcolonial African states and the historically rooted resistance to them by African revolutionary, counter-hegemonic forces. This is the subject matter of the next section of this discourse.

Notes and References

1. Okechukwu Mezu, "Poetry and Revolution in Modern Africa", in G.D. Killam, (ed) *African Writers on African Writing* (London: Heinemann, 1973), p. 104.
2. Angus Calder, "A Sense of Shame", *Busara*, Vol. II, No. 2, (1969), pp. 16-28.
3. Adrian Roscoe's position on this issue is well articulated in his "Developments in Verse" in *Uhuru's Fire: African Literature East to South* (Cambridge: Cambridge University Press, 1977), pp. 27-32.
4. D.I. Nwoga, "Obscurity and Commitment in Modern African Poetry", *African Literature Today, No. 6,* (1973).
5. See D.I. Nwoga, "Modern African Poetry: The Domestication of a Tradition", *African Literature Today No. 10* (1979); and Chinweizu et.al. "African Poetry and its Critics", Chapter 3 of *Toward the Decolonization of Africa Literature* (Enugu: Fourth Dimension, 1980).
6. Sunday Anozie, Christopher Okigbo: *Creative Rhetoric* (London: Evans, 1972) and *Structuralist Models and African Poetics*.
7. Paul Theroux, "Voices of Skull: A Study of Six African Poets", in *Introduction to African Literature* ed. Ulli Beier, (ed) (London: Longman, 1967) and "Christopher Okigbo", *Transition* 5:22 (1965).
8. Romanus Egudu, *Four Modern West African Poets* (New York: Nok Publishers, 1977), *Modern African Poetry and the African Predicament* (New York: Nok, 1978); "Modern African Poetry and Post-Colonial Politics", *Ba Shiru*, 5, No. 2 (1974); "East African Poetry: The Surprise of Its Calm", *Nigeria Magazine* Nos 10-12 (1974),

"African Literature and Social Problems", *Canadian Journal of African Studies*, 9, (1975); "Social Ataraxia in East African Poetry," *Busara*, 8, No. 1 (1976); "Defence of Culture in the Poetry of Christopher Okigbo", *African Literature Today* No 6 (1973); and "Pictures of Pain: The Poetry of Dennis Brutus", in Chris Heywood, (ed), Aspects of South African Literature (London: Heinemann, 1976).

9. Dan Izevbaye, "Death and the Artist: An Appreciation of Okigbo's Poetry", *Research in African Literatures* Vol. 13, no. 1 (1982) and "From Reality to the Dream: The Poetry of Chris Okigbo", in Edgar Wright, (ed), *The Critical Evaluation of African Literature* (London: Heinemann, 1973).

10. Donatus Nwoga, "Okigbo's Limits: An Approach to Meaning", *Journal of Commonwealth Literature*, 7.1: 92 (1969); "Religion in Modern West African Poetry", in D.I. Nwoga, (ed.), *Literature and Modern West African Culture* (Benin: Ethiope Publishers, 1978); and the already referred "Obscurity and Commitment in Modern African Poetry" and "African Poetry: The Domestication of a Tradition" See note 64.

11. G. Heron, *The Poetry of Okot P'Bitek* (London: Heinemann, 1980), and "Okot P' Bitek and the Elite in African Writing", *Literary Half-Yearly*, 19. No. 1 (1978).

12. Adrian Roscoe, *Mother is Gold* (Cambridge: Cambridge University Press, 1976) and *Uhuru's Fire*, especially Chp.2, "Development in Verse" and Chp. 3, "Aspects of South African Verse" (pp.150-167).

13. Bahadur Tejani, "Review of Okot P'Bitek's Two Songs", *African Literature Today*, No. 6 (1973); "Review of Jared Angira's Juices in *African Literature Today* No. 6 (1973); and "Can a Prisoner Make a Poet: Review of Dennis Brutus Letters to Martha", in *African Literature Today, No 6* (1973).

14. Chinweizu, et al, "Prodigals Come Home", *Okike* No. 3, Vol. 5. (1975) and *Toward the Decolonization of African Literature.*
15. Ali Mazrui, "The Patriot as an Artist", *Black Orpheus*, 2, No. 3 (1968); "Abstract Verse and African Tradition", *Zuka* no. 1 (Sept. 1967); and "Meaning and Imagery in African Poetry", *Presence Africaine* No. 66, (1966).
16. O.R. Dathorne, *African Literature in the 20th Century.* See in particular the chapter on "African Poetry in English".
17. Chukwuma Azuonye, "Christopher Okigbo and the Psychological Theories of Carl Jung", *Journal of African and Comparative Literature*, No. 1 (March, 1981).
18. See "African Poetry in English" in *African Literature in the 20th Century.*
19. Ibid., p. 183.
20. *Four Modern West African Poets,* p. xi.
21. Ibid., p. 124.
22. *Toward the Decolonization of African Literature,* pp. 193-194.
23. Quoted in above, pp. 193-194.
24. *Labyrinths* (London: Heineman, 1972), p. 32.
25. Ibid., p. 68.
26. These works are just samples of Wole Soyinka's creative efforts which clearly illustrate this transformation process. The earliest collection of Soyinka's works is in two volumes, released by Cambridge University Press.
27. Abiola Irele, "African Poetry of English Expression," *Presence Africaine* No. 57 (1966), p. 263.
28. Ulli Beier's, "Some Nigerian Poets," p. 50. Quoted in *African Literature in the 20th Century,* p. 193.
29. *African Literature in the 20th Century,* p. 193.
30. *Uhuru's Fire,* p. 32.
31. Ngugi wa Thiong'o, *Homecoming* (London: Heinemann,

1972), p. 75.
32. G.D. Killam, *African Writers on African Writing*, p. 127.
33. Term used by O.F. Onoge in "Crisis of Consciousness in African Literature; A Survey" on Senghor's brand of Negritude. The term has been explained in the textual reference and on note 27.
34. See Audu Ogbe, "38 Hours with Okot P'Bitek", *Pan African Book World*, Vol. 3 No. 2, p. 8.
35. *African Literature in the 20th Century*, p. 212.
36. G.A. Heron, *The Poetry of Okot P'Bitek*.
37. Paper presented at the 4th Annual Conference of the Literary Society of Nigeria, Benin City, Nigeria, 22-25 February, 1984.
38. "The Satire in Song of Lawino", *Horizon* 8, (1972).
39. "Lawino's Complex Protest: A Socialist Reappraisal", *Busara*, 3, No. 2 (197)
40. "Okot P'Bitek's Use of Personae: A Review of Song of Prisoner", *Benin Review* 1, (1974).
41. Okot P'Bitek: A Check List of Works and Criticism, *Research in African Literature* Vol. 16, No. 3 (1985) and "The Image of a Prostitute: A Reconsideration of P'Bitek's Malaya", *Kunapipi* (1986).
42. "Review of Okot P'Bitek's Two Songs, *African Literature Today*, No. 6 (1973).
43. "Okot P'Bitek and the Elite in East African Writing," *Literary Half Yearly*, and "Dissecting P'Bitek," *East African Journal*, 8, 8 (1971).
44. "Okot P' Bitek: Writer, Singer, Culturizer," in *Standpoints on African Literature*. Chris Wanjala (ed) (Nairobi: East African Literature Bureau, 1973).
45. "Okot P'Bitek and Writing in East Africa" in *Homecoming* (London: Heinemann, 1972).
46. "Okot P'Bitek: Literature and Cultural Revolution", *Journal of African Studies*, Vol. 5, No. 3 (1978).

47. "Four Songs of African Dilemma by Okot P' Bitek", *Current Bibliography on African Affairs*, 8, (1973).
48. "Modes of Freedom: The Songs of Okot P'Bitek," *Journal of Commonwealth Literature*, XV, 1 (Aug. 1980).
49. "Song of Prisoner: A reply to Atieno-Odhiambo," *Busara*, Vol. 4, No. 1, (1972).
50. "Okot P'Bitek" in Cosmo Pieterse and D. Munro, eds. *African Writers Talking* (London: Heinemann, 1972).
51. "Okot P'Bitek and the Rise of East African Writing" in Bruce King and K. Ogungbesan, eds. *A Celebration of Black and African Writing* (Ibadan: Univ. Press; Zaria: Ahmadu Bello University Press, 1975).
52. See *Uhuru's* Fire, pp. 76-84.
53. "Discovering East African Poets," in *East African Literature: An Anthology* ed. Ane Zettersten (London: Longman, 1983), p. 222.
54. "A postscript on 8 Poems", *Busara*, Vol.1, No. 1, (1968), p. 35.
55. "Jared Angira: Committed Experimental Poet" in *Individual and Commitment in Commonwealth Literature*, ed., Daniel Massa (Malta: Old University Press, 1979), P. 37
56. "Jared Angira," in *Uhuru's Fire*, p. 94.
57. "Jared Angira and East African Poetry of Social Testimony," *World Literature Written in English*, Vol. 23, No. 2 (Spiring 1984), p. 328.
58. "Jared Angira: Review of Juices," *African Literature Today, No.6* (1973), p. 159.
59. "East African Poetry, "*African Literature Today, No. 6*, p. 52.
60. "Preface", *Juices* (Nairobi: EAPH, 1970), pp. 7-8.
61. Ezenwa-Ohaeto, "Black Consciousness in East/South African Poetry: Unity and Divergence in the Poetry of Taban Lo Liyong and Sipho Sepamla", *Presence*

Africaine, No. 140 (4th Quarterly, 1986), and "The Poetic Experimentation in Taban Lo Liyong's Franz Fanon's Uneven Ribs", *Journal of English Studies,* Vol. 111 (Sept. 1986).
62. "Seasons of Omen," in *Casualties*: Poem 1966/68 (London: Longman Group Ltd, 1970), pp. 11-12.
63. R.N. Egudu, "Poetry as an Inquiry into the Meaning of Life," Inaugural Lecture Delivered at the University of Benin, Benin City, May, 1982, p. 22.
64. Ibid., p. 24.
65. In *Satellites* (London: Heinemann, 1967), pp. 80-90.
66. Contained in *Poems from East Africa* ed. D. Cook and D. Rubadiri (London: Heinemann, 1971), p. 49.
67. See Socialist Realism and the Modern Literary Process, Chapter 5. And Socialist Literatures: "Problems of Development," Chapter 6 for the transitional nature of critical realism.

Part Four

ART AND IDEOLOGY IN THE PERIOD OF RE-COLONIZATION: THE REVOLUTIONARY AESTHETIC IMPERATIVE

What can one say about the poetry of the late 1970s, 1980s and 1990s in Africa? For one, a careful study of the poetic experimentation of the period will reveal a clear, qualitative ideo-aesthetic break from the critical realist poetry of the 1960s and early 1970s, except in the sustenance of the latter Okigbo oracular tradition enunciated in his "Path of Thunder" sequences. The concept of re-colonization interpreted in the lexicon of modern African socio-political and socio-cultural usage and experience, needs no clarification here. The contradictions of the current epoch, the tremendous social changes going on in Africa and the fundamental impact of the world democratic process in the continent are image-making imperatives from where the new revolutionary poets draw their creative impetuses.

What is of course, certain about the new poets of "alternative tradition",[1] to use Funso Aiyejina's term is that they are essentially ideological combatants, positing new visions and ideals about an acceptable democratic, humanistic and people-oriented mode of production and structure of social relation, through an innovative and refreshing socio-aesthetic means. Variously called the "avantgardists", the "revolutionary experimenters" and the "iconoclasts", their works are deeply rooted in the tradition of struggle, and are highly influenced by an admixture of Leftist ideologies that range from neo-Marxism-Leninism to African communalism/socialism.

Differentiating the combative poets of the 1980s and 1990s from the poets of the 60s is basically simple, both on the purely aesthetic score of poetic manner and the idea-content that undergirds poetic matter. While the older poets explore experience and social reality with a highly distorted privatist idiom (excepting P'Bitek, Awoonor and the later Okigbo); while they experiment with a quasi-modernist form of oblique allusions, personal imageries and myths, obscure references and difficult inter-textual borrowings of essentially elliptical nature; and while they permutated language in a manner that substantially destroys its organic link and inter-connection with objective reality because of the pursuit of esoteric meaning and individualistic, personalized and subjectivist essences,[2] the revolutionary poets adopt a public medium and re-discover the vital strategies of traditional poetic modes of articulation and delivery: chants, songs, sound accompaniment, incantations and all the various structures of verbal art forms, including proverbs, curses, praises, insults and poetic anecdotes to capture the dynamics of existence in a virtually re-colonized continent striving towards self-awareness. The language of the poetry is vibrant and charged, and is replete with imagistic patterns and innovative symbolic associations of diverse implicatur.

In social concern too, we readily discover that while they sometimes handle the themes already explored by the older poets, they do so from the perspective of new knowledge, new consciousness and a better understanding of the dialectics of social change. They are more socially minded, politically committed, optimistic, deeply concerned about social amelioration and willing to set clear solutions to the dominant social contradictions of the current epoch. When they adopt a reflective attitude in their poems, or betray a clear bitterness and revulsion at the ugliness of living in a society mutilated by atavistic values, they do so with a visible intent to caricature and condemn, and thereby point the way forward, but never in the cynical, mocking, and existentially despairing manner noticeable in some of the critical realist poets of the 1960s.

There are an appreciable number of poets who have emerged in the period under survey, and who are the successors to other slightly undifferentiated breed of poets who appeared like meteors in the early 1970s, with some of them either silenced by creative drought or are still taking stock of the poetic scene before staging a creative comeback. One or two are regrettably dead, like the late Paul Ndu who many critics believe was poised to take over from where Chris Okigbo left off.[3] For example, recent researches by discerning scholars in Nigeria, have demonstrated the emergence of a poetic tradition at University of Nigeria, Nsukka immediately after the war, a tradition initiated by people like Obiora Udechuwku and Chukwuma Azuonye and which, at least, in the vibrancy of the language and the anti-establishment consciousness that imbues it, makes the experiment ideo-aesthetically close to the poetry of the late 1970s, 1980s and early 1990s.[4] D.I. Nwoga, in his already mentioned "Modern African Poetry: The Domestication of a Tradition" gives attention to the young poets of the early 1970s who are mostly influenced by Okigbo and Soyinka but some of who are on the threshold of discovering and developing their own individual poetic voices.[5]

One can say that in Nigeria, at least, the real signal of revolutionary and avant-gardism poetry was sounded by Odia Ofeimun, a long time contributor to the *Okike Journal*, and who has attracted attention in the Nwoga and Maduakor studies long before his notable collection, *The Poet Lied* came out. Also, writing at the same time with Ofeimun or even shortly before him (only a close personalized research can date their earliest published poem) is Chinweizu, whose *Energy Crisis and Other Poems* came out in 1977 and which constitutes a transitional phase in the transformation of critical realism into revolutionary art. His much later award-winning collection, *Admonitions and Invocations,* containing the brilliant sequence, "Lament of the Dauntless Three", is truly central to the tradition we are discussing here. Yet Chinweizu, as a poet, is so contradictory, so torn apart by disparate forces, and so committed, almost fanatically and obsessively, to an amorphous Pan-African vision that we do not consider him a true candidate of revolutionary aesthetic sensibility in modern Nigerian poetry.

It is important to point out here that the present researcher does not make any pretensions about any special knowledge of contemporary West African poetry, not to talk of contemporary African poetry in general. So the discussion in this section is essentially and regrettably localized to just Nigeria where, fortunately, we have enough voices to warrant a tentative probing. Nevertheless, I strongly feel that, apart from the newness of the poets in the field, (some have only published a collection or two), which may even make the charge of hasty and inconclusive critical attention real, the tendency discernible in Nigeria is also underscorable in other parts of Africa because of a near uniformity of contemporary socio-political and socio-economic experience (check for example the reality of political instability, coup d'état, mass poverty, and the continental reach and spread of IMF and World Bank pills of structural adjustment economic programmes, liberal capitalist democratization processes, etc).

In Nigeria, some members of the "older" generation of the revolutionary poets whose poetic modes and social concerns clearly demonstrate the charting of a new poetic tradition, and a new alternative sensibility are Niyi Osundare, easily the best poet to emerge out of Nigeria, if not Africa, after Okigbo (*Songs of the Marketplace, Village Voices, Moon Song, The Eye of the Earth* – which won the Commonwealth poetry prize – and *A Nib in the Pond*): Harry Garuba (*Shadows and Dreams*); Tanure Ojaide, (*Labyrinths of the Delta*), and Ezenw-Ohaeto, (*Songs of a Traveller, I Wan Bi President* and *Bullet for Buntings*). The new voices that have been added are quite extensive and many more are getting published. Among the younger generation of the new combative singers, who are already sounding more confident and self-assured than their older revolutionary compatriots, are Esiaba Irobi (*Frozen Music, Handgrenades* and *Cotyledons*); Emman Usman Shehu (*Questions for Big Brother*); Uche Nduka (*Flower Child*); Afam Akeh (*Stolen Moments*); Idzia Ahmad (*A Shout Across the Wall*); and Kenvi Atanda Ilori (*Amnesty*).

For the purposes of this tentative incursion into an area still relatively virgin, [6] we will take a close look at Ezenwa-Ohaeto's *Songs of a Traveller* and Niyi Osundare's *Songs of the Market Place* and *The Eye of the Earth*. Attention will, nevertheless, be focused on some of the collections already mentioned, but the substantial ingredients of our discussion will emanate from the collections of Ohaeto and Osundare as exemplifiers of the ideo-aesthetic tendencies we have been scrutinizing, and as representative of that essentially oracular, traditionalist – communalist poetic craft associated with societies pre-dating colonial imperialism.

Songs of a Traveller[7] could be read as an astonishing amalgam of apparently disparate currents and tendencies struggling for poetic focus and foregrounding. One detects now a quiet, resonant voice of courage, endurance and fortitude; a sharp, alarmingly hysterical and shrill call for change, for radical readjustment of values and a fundamental overhauling of the establishment, delivered through a satiric mode that is illustrative of the poet's revulsion and disgust at the social barbarism of the ruling class; an almost frightening degeneration into sheer alienation, a compelling loss of belief and faith and an iconoclastic disinterestedness that sometimes bothers on desperate nihilism; and then, a sequence of *Orikis* for "kindred spirits". What can we make out of this apparently "disjointed" and "shocking" blending of several, sometimes contradictory ideas? Poetic immaturity or defective vision? No. Carefully approached, the collection reveals an internal order, an inner organic logic and dialectical correlation of ideas and thoughts that demonstrate the poet's reverence of humanism, his abhorrence of ineptitude, corruption, tyranny and the stranglehold of re-colonizing imperialism, and a courageous resistance to depression and disillusionment.

The clarion note of combat and challenge is sounded in the very first poem, "A Song in the Morning", where the guerilla speaker prepares for a journey of confrontation with the adverse forces of inhumanity with this rallying call:

> Gather the Garments
> Let us set out now
> With songs to break down walls
> Where hammers remain powerless (p. 1)

This defiant note is sustained throughout the poem and is extended imaginatively into the second song, "A New Kind of Song", a name suggestive of a break with the poetic tradition and social concerns of "past songs" in modern African poetry.[8] At the end of the poem, we realize that the poet's songs are:

> Songs breathing fumes of fury
> Exuding sad fumes of bitterness
> For the rage wells up in me
> If I cannot sing to your ears
> Just let me hum to myself (p. 2)

The ground has, therefore, been tilled for the full unleashing of righteous poetic fury on the potpourri gathering of politicians, military bigwigs, academics, businessmen and bureaucratic elite who have turned the society into one giant trading company where they hold controlling shares. The poems that readily yield to this level of interpretation are "A Song for the Drummers", "Song of an Unemployed", "A Song for Nigeria", "Song of a Beggar" and "Song of a Drought". In "A Song for the Drummers", drummers here assuming a highly symbolic status as troupe accompaniment and not as a central part of instrumental assemblage, is a passionate assessment of the role of hypocrites and sycophants who help in the institutionalization of official corruption and moral depravity, and who are spiritually drained, hollow and unsatisfied. They are:

> A conglomeration of contractors
> A handful of public servants
> A sprinkling of devious academics (p.7)

Who, "After the long carnival" of hedonism, are shown as frail, tried and forgotten.

The "Song of an Unemployed" and "Song of a Beggar" are bitter satires of the contradictory social relations in a re-colonized society, where the few members of the ruling class revel in an uninhibited display of filthy wantonness while the mass of the people wallow in destitution and neglect and are stupefied by ignorance and disease. The unemployed, probably a graduate, laments about his shoes that "caress/the jagged stoned of the streets"/his "eyes devouring the potent pages of newspapers"/and his fingers "tracing the contours of application forms" only to be informed that "in the prevailing circumstances/A vacancy no longer exists")" (p.8). The beggar, on his own part, rejected and cast off to the fringe of alienated social living, slum-dwelling and ghetto sub-culture; in short, to the desolate waste of the "murky waters of the gutter", discovers that he is damned, for

> At what times does
> The tear become a laugh?
> At what stage do the dumb
> Beckon thunder to speak for them?
> At what period do the blind
> Ask the lightning to see for them?
> At what point do the deaf

Ask rain to hear for them (p. 9)

Surely, all these situations are fantastic; they only exist as happenstances in the "fertile" imagination of the lost. They are all indicative of the apparent immutability of the content and patterns of socio-economic experience in a re-colony like Nigeria.

"A Song for Nigeria," decrying Nigeria's twenty-five years of nationhood which is characterized by political ineptitude, acrimonious social upheavals and enduring instability, re-colonial dependency and social reaction, is one of the most bitter pieces in the entire collection. In the poem, executed with an elegiac elegance, the poet laments that the fate of the nation is a "tale of wounded emotions"/and "a tale of broken hearts." Not daunted by this and the harrowing fact that "a committee of elders could/become a committee of murderers", his defiance and courage break out in this sequence:

> It may be difficult to speak
> It is impossible to be silent
> For ripples turn into a tide
> In a cloud of fear bred by terror (p. 10)

Cosmetic measures which may assume the form and shape of coup d'état, feeble-minded democratic reformism and vain glorious call for moral rearmament proffer no solutions. What we need, the poet asserts, is a clean break, a total and fundamental re-ordering of priorities based on an entirely new socio-economic structure, for the earlier cosmetic measures are "changing faces" and "not fortunes", "changing hatred" but not "bringing hopes. At the end, the poet, who assumes a prophetic role, admonishes that unless this is done the "fire next time/... may consume even the air" (p. 11).

The naïve belief that once the military come to power through a coup d'état, society experiences regeneration, rebirth and national awakening is profoundly false in relation to the class structure of developing countries. What actually happens is that the top military brass who constitute the dominant arm of the Repressive State Apparatuses of the political ruling class, feeling that an inept civilian government which is thoroughly discredited and rejected, will leave the room open for popular rebellion that could lead to the revolutionary transformation of society, quickly move to fill the vacuum, sustain and perpetuate the status quo, enrich themselves many times over and end up more barbarous, corrupt and inept than the regime it has sacked. Experience in Nigeria, in particular, has shown that virtually all the emergency millionaires in the country were produced in the 1970-1999 period, a time in which the military was in power for twenty-five years out of the twenty-nine years. This is what Ezenwa-Ohaeto seems to be saying in "Oriki of a General" and "Song of a Labourer" (*If to Say I Bi Soja*).

The two poems are uncompromising and scathing in their criticism of the role of the military in the apparatus of state power; the undemocratic and tyrannical base of their governance; and their corruption and mismanagement of national resources. The stealthy and surreptitious way they capture power is clearly demonstrated in "Oriki of a General":

> Welcome to the throne of bayonets
> You now sent forth mysterious fears
> In an early morning shower of bullets
> For a general is in change (p. 27)

The unfettered way the soldiers loot the state treasury and the evidence of that plunder come out forcefully when we notice that their "cheeks have filled out" and that "their stomachs have ballooned." Added to these is the fact that the general (in charge) is the:

> Owner of foreign bank accounts
> Controller of fishing trawlers
> Manager of complete companies
> Land speculator in several states (p. 27)

The unpopularity of the general's government, its anti-people stance and fascist disposition are captured thus:

> The harbinger of heavy decrees
> The promulgator of ailing edicts
> The detector of complex coup plots
> Welcome to the General in charge (p. 27)

"The Song of a Labourer", a very original poem, written in Nigerian Pidgin English, continues the argument initiated in the preceding poem. Using the simple instance of a labourer who fails in his bid to marry a girl of his choice because the lady wants a soldier-husband, the poet launches into a wide-ranging satire on the entire military institution. For one thing, the soldiers are a special breed of people unaffected by the prevailing socio-economic stresses and pressures that weigh the ordinary man down. If he were to be a soldier, the labourer ruminates everything would have been fine for him. He laments.

> Retirement no for worry me
> Retrenchment no for trouble me
> Irregular pay no for harass me
> Police no go ask wetin I carry
> Thief no go ask wetin I get
> Tax man no go ask wetin bi my salary (p. 30)

To show that the soldiers are no better than the politicians, the poetic persona states that if he is a soldier "I go make/ decree say all better house/go dey my Papa compound/I for don make edict wey go make my Mama farm/one better palace so/Na Switzerland for be kitchen/for my own million Billion Naira" (p. 31). That is not all. If he is a soldier, definitely his brother will be made a minister; his friend, a board chairman; and his houseboy will equally get a job as a permanent secretary. The basic task, therefore, for a soldier in power is to satisfy the interests of his cohorts as against the wider aspirations and needs of the rest of society. Reality eventually dawns on the persona-dreamer when he realizes that all his wishful thinking will come to naught for "I no be Soja. And my mouth no be gun" (p. 31).

Speaking about the soldier, we are reminded of what Leo Tolstoy said about military service and life in general. That assertion is important here, for it points out the psyche of the military man and seems to illustrate the rationale for most of his actions. Tolstoy wrote that:

> Military service always corrupts a man, placing him in conditions of complete idleness, that is, absence of all intelligent and useful work, and liberating him from the common obligations of humanity, for which it substitutes conventional considerations like the honour of the regiment, the uniform and the flag, and, on the one hand, investing him with unlimited power over men and on the other, demanding slavish subjection to superior officers.[9]

Even in such poems as "Song of a Coward," which has a striking similarity with Martin Niemoeller's "To the Faculty,"[10] which celebrates despair, deflation of spirit, social alienation and "passive indifference" to oppression and "mute complicity" to organized brutality, to borrow Franz Fanon's terms, we still find an indirect echo of humanism and a self-critical outlook that salvages the tattered dignity of the persona. The coward is not bothered when the fanatics "decimated the people,"/chasing the mumbling Moslems"/ and "pursuing the croaking Christians" because he has no religion. His indifference continues when it is the turn of the journalist to be jailed, the children to be "sent out of school," and when the entire family of father, mother, son and daughter are made to taste one bitter pill of oppression or another. Like all passive people, it becomes too late for him to act when he is made to experience the same brutality for there is no ally left:

> Now a noose woven strong
> Tightens round my scrawny neck
> My eyes bulge in terror

My tongue rolls out
I want to weep
But tears are no more (pp. 4-5)

"Song of a Coward" underscores a tendency that starts with the suppression of religious groups and professionals (Moslems, Christians and journalists) and degenerates into a coordinated attack on all the people, irrespective of race, religion and ideological and political persuasion (the brutalization of the whole family). The situation here is more alarming and lamentable than what obtains in Neimoeller's poem[11] because while the Nazi butchers made token concessions to the German Aryans, some of whom supported their policies, the government in Ohaeto's poem seems to have declared war on all the people. This is a classic case of a historically progressive policy of destruction, from selective genocide to a doctrine of total extermination.

But what is particularly of interest is the position of the persona in the poem. He feels alienated from and disinterested in the horror around him because, at its commencement, his individual freedom and sense of humanity have not been violated. When eventually the terror catches up with him, there is nobody to give him succour and refuge. The poem, therefore, seems to state that one is duty-bound to oppose oppression whether one is directly affected or not, for not to do so is surely a preparation for one's own ruination. In a way, then, the persona's self-criticism and recognition of the tragedy of his inaction is an indirect statement of his commitment to humanity, an indication of his late realization of the need to be a decisive combatant, and a warning to those alive not to follow his isolationist footsteps. Therein lies his regeneration and humanism.

I Wan Bi President,[12] Ezenwa-Ohaeto's second collection of poems in "formal and pidgin English" is a highly incisive piece that boldly takes on the whole wide-ranging and complex structures of decadent social and political institutions in Nigeria's postcolonial moment. Nothing is spared in the whole poetic design of ridicule and biting caricature. Subjecting the history of Nigeria to an acute dialectical scrutiny, the poet underscores the inevitability of revolutionary social change as a necessary outcome of the contradictions engendered by an inhuman and inequitable mode of material production and structure of social relations. From phrase-mongers and ideological sloganeers; and from makers of myth and upholders of obscurantist philosophies parading as revolutionary paradigms of social transformation to the flatulent elite, emergency contractors and irresponsible military officers, especially those operating at the highest levels of government, the poet sends a profound message of their ultimate annihilation and achieves redemption for his society, basically on the context of his faith in revolutionary social change.

Poems like "Let Us Have a Dialogue", in which the poet laments the lack of communication as a consequence of the social blindness and moral deafness of his generation, because, regrettably, "these fellow athletes/chanting revolutionary songs (are) indoctrinated with shallow rhetoric," is an example of a very critical poem in the collection whose comprehensive negation of the social formation is saved from being mere critical realism by the underpinning humanism and revolutionary ideal ascribed to the quest. Other poems worthy of note as socio-political items of commentary, analysis and proposition are "The Inquisitive Idiot", "Them Go Tell the President" and "Fingers no Equal."

But it is in "I wan Bi president," a highly satirical poem, composed in Nigerian Pidgin English, and cast in the mode of a dream-revelation, and which is very similar to "Song of a Labourer" in *Songs of a Traveller* that Ohaeto projects his complete vision of a wasted generation, and a social system that is unjust and inhuman. The ironic structures of the poem are very intricate and subtle and even indict the 'poetic persona', and probably by extension, the poet, of reactionary and conservative tendencies, of the willingness and readiness to participate in the socially annihilating process of national waste and ruin. This is because the persona doesn't seem to quarrel with the basis of corruption and exploitation and sees them as attributes he aspires to. He is content to enjoy the trappings of power and wishes fervently that he occupies that position.

But this mode of reading over-simplifies the poem's aesthetic ontology. The poem is a negation of the principle underlying the very concept of autocracy, and an uncompromising criticism of the corruptibility of power. In the apparent self-effacing naivety of the persona is underpinned the fundamental social phenomenon of false consciousness engendered by an ideological persuasion that is made rapacious and potent by its dominant material basis. The ideas of the ruling class being the ruling ideas in every epoch, it becomes perfectly possible for the persona, as a socio-politically conditioned subject, to aspire to the material level associated with the presidency because of the reflection in his distorted and corrupted consciousness, the very essence of that material state. The president, for example, is never hungry, thirsty and dirty, and neither does he drive a car himself nor travel in a congested road. The president doesn't push truck:

> From morning reach for night
> Even if e no find ten kobo chop
> I never see president go home
> With hoe wey don spoil finish
> Na him make I wan bi president (p. 35)

It is not only the president who benefits from his special position. The material condition of members of his family, his servants and cohorts is an indication of their closeness to power and centre of authority – political and economic. His servant, we are told, "dey eat well well," his wife "go dey smile as e dey happy" while "na guard go dey" follow his children, giving them maximum security and protection.

After this enumeration of the material benefits accruable to the president's immediate family, the persona-dreamer launches into a wide-ranging satire of the different categories of presidents that exist. We are made aware of the existence of life presidents, presidents who, though they have never won election, still cling tenaciously to power, and some presidents who never lose election, scoring a minimum of 99% of the votes any time election is organized. It is not even the very fact of unwillingness to relinquish power that characterizes the absolute and authoritarian powers of such presidents, nor their selfish desire to uplift their communities, materially and socially, at the expense of the other parts of the nation that equally deserve his attention, but the very fact of megalomania, arrogation of despotic powers and obsession with recognition and self pride. Thus, the persona-dreamer

> ... Wan bi president
> Make I get plenty titles
> Dey go call me de Excellency
> I go bi Commander-in-Chief
> I fit be Field Marshall and Admiral
> I go bi Lion of de Niger
> I go answer Grand Commander of de Nation,
> Dem go address me as snake wey get forest, (p. 38)

Not even the realization that he has been indulging in wishful thinking, in an unrealistic dream, could reduce the potency of the persona's charge against the corruptibility and, later on, inevitable destructibility of power. "I wan Bi President", the poem, achieves its socio-aesthetic significance not just in the area of language experimentation, but also in the already stated issues of exposing, as a way of ameliorating, the odious practices in most African countries, committed by the highest authority in the land: the President.

The persistent feeling that emerges after a reading of Ezenwa-Ohaeto's poetry in the two collections, especially those directly relevant to the issue of ideology, is that, despite the fact that some of them have a unifying thematic standpoint or idea-content, the same intensity of feeling and emotional equilibrium, and, therefore, could be isolated for separate consideration, the fact remains that all the poems have an internal order, a central vision, a basic thrust: to be a combatant, a vigorous fighter for humanity and positive motivator of change, a lot of difficulties must be encountered and setbacks endured, but these should never force one to give up, to desert the ranks of the people, for in deeds of great and enduring verity, personal safety is the least of all considerations.

Niyi Osundare's *Songs of the Marketplace* deserves a place in the development of modern African poetry. Lyrical, mellifluous and highly imagistic and sometimes incantatory (a sign of his knowledge of and familiarity with traditional verbal art forms), the collection shows the poet's acute consciousness about the content and structure of living in a society that values mediocrity, socio-political drift, oppression and exploitation. The poet's ideo-aesthetic standpoint is much more than a mere criticism of existing reality; he posits a positive vision that it is only through a revolutionary and progressive re-orientation of society and a fundamental revaluation of mores and beliefs that a new humanistic and people-oriented dispensation can emerge. Poems like "Excursions", "Sule Chase", "Given", "Publish or Perish", "Udorji" and "I Sing of Change" are some of the pieces that celebrate the poet's dauntless commitment to exposing the ugliness of living, and that establish his steadfastness to moral and political integrity.

"Excursions" is a poetic representation of the variegated essences of living in a society that cherishes all the basest elements of existence. It reveals the depth of material deprivation, poverty and alienation of the individual from the polity and the machinations of the wealthy and the powerful in their sustained bid to oppress and exploit the masses. The poem is divided into four parts. Part one, lets us into the world of people with "sunken eyes", babies "squeezing spongy breasts," and village boys with "kwashiokored bellies" and "hairless heads". We also see that "the family head to the bush trapping rats and insects" and that in "city fringes pregnant women rummage in garbage heaps/for the rotting remnants of city tables", while above, "hawks and vultures hover(ing) for their turn" (pp. 7-8). The images change in quick successive patterns and reveal an anguished farmer torturing a tired soil with rusty primitive implements, transient labourers dripping bucketfuls of sweat for a miserable day pay while an ever-lengthening crowd queue querulously before a lottery office.

The second to the last picture created in the first section of the poem is that of religious frenzy in a mushroom drum-beating church. It tells a lot about the material and spiritual condition of the people. In circumstances of dire financial and economic disability and frustration quasi-religious zealotry and pseudo-mystical enthusiasm become the sustaining imperative of existence. The spread of factionalized and factionalizing sects with their epiphanic visions that 'occur' everyday and the exulted religious imagination of fanatics who increase by the thousands every minute are all indicative of the spiritual crisis created by excruciating socio-economic conditions. That is why, in the poem "The Neighbourhood Church:"

> The faithful sing into
> Catatonic orgasms,
> Hymning and psalming are the diet
> Of the soul though the body succumbs
> To the buffets of hunger
> Between belches the plump preacher
> Extols the virtue of want,
> The only ticket to the wealth beyond (p. 9)

It is, of course, not surprising that while the members of the congregation are in dire need of food, the preacher is "pump" and "belches" out his flatulence. This is the logic of the law of spiritual enslavement which breeds false consciousness and rationalizes exploitation and greed.

The second part of the poem, continuing the same sequences of imagistic presentation, takes us to the world of the beggars, some of who are "victims of our recent war" and "battered grass in the battle/of mindless elephants" and who line our common route presenting the picture of "running sore of broken humanity." Some of them "crawl like crabs," while "many have limbs and eyes and ears/only beggared by unceasing lay-offs/handy jettisons of captains of industry". The persona's moral conclusion, borne out of a profound reflection on the nature of poverty, is that:

> These sightless sockets
> Bore indictory gazes into
> Heavy pockets
> And vaults of hoarded loot
> These swinging stumps
> Are pointers to
> The skulls behind our corpulent grins (p. 11)

The third and final part of "Excursions" drives further home the point of general social decay and mental stupor, and the deliberate attempt to cultivate and institutionalize the culture of exploitation, national waste and re-colonial dependency to foreign capitalist and imperialist interests. We have the persistent images of workers who, as purveyors of the consciousness and ideas generated by their bosses, ensure that files are lost and found by "mysterious magic." There are also the ever increasing files on the boss's tray, and the street whisper of the commoners about millions of Naira salted away in foreign banks by the nation's rulers. In universities, students line the corridors talking:

> About threadbare gurus
> Recycling worn traditions
> Dreading change like despots...
> Pawning wives for chairs
> Then slinking into glamorized mediocrity
> Breeding flat minds
> Diplomated with the slavish stamp

Of received gospels (p.13)

Having confronted us with these pictures of decay and the more sordid one of rulers ensconced in fortressed palaces and ruling by boot and butt, the poet breaks forth in an incantatory sequence that highlights the dialectics of nature, his revolutionary hope and enthusiasm, and his belief about the inevitable triumph of progress and freedom. He captures this powerfully in the following lines:

> But soon
> The people will shout
> When murmurs break through muzzles
> And will powers into action
> Oppression's cloud will clear
> The sun eastering hence
> A life full and free (p. 15)

The same basic contradiction of existence and the same dichotomy between the minority rich and powerful and the majority neglected and alienated is captured in the poem, "Siren" (Music of the Visiting Power). The poem underscores the insensitivity and indifference of touring state leaders who expect "kwashiokored children" to wave "tattered flags/ in the baking sun," when they have forfeited the day's meal, and "orchestrated cultural dancers" to drip "drums of sweat" in entertaining them. These are the demands of the visiting powers as sop to their ego and megalomania, for surely they have no time:

> For dry days
> And dark nights
> Or food whose price
> Costs a ton of gold
> No time for hospitals
> And schools and roads... (p. 22)

But as in "Excursions", the poet does not subscribe to the philosophy of fatalism and social annihilation; neither does he believe in the immutability and pemanency of oppression and exploitation. He knows that questions are bound to be asked and many will be poised to not only raise objections but also precipitate the collapse of such an inhuman order. It is in the very nature and structure of oppression that its requiem song is emblematized thus:

> But babies contorted
> In mothers' backs
> Are question marks
> For tomorrows answer (p. 23)

We have already mentioned that several other of Osundare's poems in *Songs of the Market place* and several of the poems in his later collections like *The Eye of the Earth* and *Moon Songs* mediate a decadent but turbulent and transformational political and social reality in a manner yet unmatched by any other temporary Nigerian and, probably, African poet. Of course, an analysis of these other collections will afford us further and deeper insight into Osundare's art and his creative use of socio-political and ideological parameters to capture the essences of existence in their progressive development. But we are strongly persuaded that the two poems analyzed above have thrown sufficient light on his main poetic concern, as it pertains to art and ideology, and will stimulate further research and discussion on the use of artistic, and essentially, imagistic forms and patterns of signification in modern Nigerian poetry to locate the possibility of the revolutionary transformation of society.

We will round-up the discussion on this section by looking at the already named group of Nigerian revolutionary and combative poets as a way of suggesting what could be the main direction of their art.

Uche Nduka (*Flower Child*) [13] is still young and one can detect the urgency and idealism of youth in his poetry. The language of the poems in the collection is vibrant and emotive and deeply replete with enthusiastic outbursts, either in the eulogization of positive social tendencies or the censuring of socially and morally-debasing elements in the society. Already, one can determine the evolving poetic style of the young artist who seems to favour imagistic patterns of signification and incantatory and invocatory devices that are sometimes laced with contemplative and reflective diction. There is no doubt that Uche Nduka is acutely aware of the social forces at work in the society, neither is there doubt, too, that he is assuredly on the side of the oppressed majority, the 80% of the people living below the poverty line.

His revolutionary romanticism, which is a healthy ideo-aesthetic vision, blends organically with his sobering and calculative mediation of the historical and socio-political forces that have turned postcolonial Nigeria into a tattered and beggared state. Poems such as "Bruises", "Revolution", "In the Streets", "Anthem" and "Drowning Voices" are very significant in this direction, though they are by no means the only politically committed poems in the collection. "Bruises" reveals the pathetic condition of social stupor, ineptitude and indecision, when people seem incapacitated and mentally in-alert to the scourge of oppression. They can only leave "Pawmarks/ of our bruises in the sun" when they are apparently left alone on the "tidal creek" but

> Over the edge
> Over the mighty edge
> (We) Wave the fronds of indecision (p. 2)

This balancing act between the idea of unity and disjunction, harmony and disorder, action and inaction is continued in the other mentioned poems, except "Revolution" and "In the Streets" where the poet manifests his revolutionary vision and shows that the people can take control of their destiny. "In the Streets" is a highly prophetic and incantatory poem that is cast in the mold of Okigbo's "Path of Thunder". Making use of sound elements and suggestive expressions that extend the possibility of meaning the poet celebrates the inevitability of radical change and the expected wave of positive social upheaval that will fundamentally alter the structure and content of material existence. This is captured thus:

> Here the clouds
> Are sea-beds fingered
> By the Sun
>
> Chants from the sky
> Showering the foliage:
>
> Brother, there is mutiny
> Under the clouds
> A plague in the streets.

The mutiny is against the oppressors, after they have been scourged by plentiful plagues let loose by the people's anger. This is essentially the message of the poem and in it is crated Nduka's stand about the Nigerian condition.

Emman Usman Shehu's Questions for Big Brother[14] is similar to Uche Nduka's *Flower Child* because of the social concern shown in a great number of the poems in the collection. If anything, Usman Shehu is even more open, trenchant and direct in his attack on dysfunctional social institutions, on revolutionary inaction, on oppression and on the expected hope of a free tomorrow. "Hands Worth Revolution", "Songs of My People" and "Questions for Big Brother" are some of the poems that contain substantial dose of social commentary. "Hands Worth Revolution" is an exhortatory poem that laments the complacency and apathy of a great number of the oppressed people. This anti-social tendency is normally borne out of false consciousness, ignorance and lack of awareness of the true material forces at work in society. The oppressed, the poet seems to be saying, will remain in their oppressed condition unless they awaken from their stupor, take their destiny in their hands and confront the inhuman forces that weigh them down and destroy their humanity. The poem is a further extension of Franz Fanon's message to the youth of Africa: "The future will have no pity for those of us who, possessing the exceptional ability to speak words of truth to the oppressor, have instead taken refuge in an attitude of passivity, mute indifference and sometimes of cold complicity."[15]

In the poem, the speaker asks "sister", "brother", "mother" and "father" what their hands are worth when they "sit on... backside"/"and state, and stare, and stare" and are "benumbed by crushing blows"/"deadened by treacherous blows"/"along the way of sorrow" (p. 28). After the repetition of "what are your hands worth", the speaker states unequivocally that such hands are worthless when they cannot fight off:

> Lethargy (that) dangles down your neck
> Like a milestone
> Silence stifles your vocal chord
> Like a brimstone
> Complacency chokes your reasoning
> Like a blank wall,
> Apathy deadens your purpose
> Like a deadweight
> And you sit and stare
> And do not dare
> To raise your hands and cuff
> Links of oppression. (p. 29)

In criticizing the people's weaknesses, and pointing out their failings and limitations, the poet is, of course, preparing them for a revolutionary challenge against the system through the creation of the necessary consciousness and class solidarity. As a negation of nihilism and social annihilation, the ideo-aesthetic imperative of the poem suggests strongly that the future holds out bright promise only if the downtrodden can understand the laws of history and use them to their benefit and advantage. This is the recurring motif in Shehu's poetry, as shown again in "Song of My People" in which he underscores the universality of oppression and the internationalism of class solidarity:

> Hunger knows no tribe,

> Hunger knows no manhood,
> Hunger knows no decrees,
> Hunger knows no gallery playing
> ("Song of My People") p. 35

In "Questions for Big Brother," he celebrates the defiance of the stubborn and tenacious fighter for justice by reminding "Big Brother" that brute force can never make him give up the fight against man's inhumanity to man:

> You can drag me
> But can you force me to drink
>
> You place me under hammer
> But will bringing it down bend my will?
>
> You run circles round my convictions
> But can you prise off my grip? (p. 67)

It is this tendency to exhort the people, reinforce their spirit and embolden them into action; this tendency to stress the positive gains of struggle and challenge; and this tendency of celebrating moments of revolutionary heroism, defiance, courage and steadfastness that map the main ideo-aesthetic contours of Usman Shehu's poetry, and point at its future direction and development.

Kemi Atanda Ilori in *Amnesty*[16] demonstrates a conscious understanding of the dynamics of social processes and a willingness to participate in evolving a progressive society through effecting fundamental changes. His poems are sometimes as intensely political as Usman Shehu's and sometimes as incantatory as Uche Nduka's. His poetry is a subtle blend of social and political commentary and artistic imagination in a near subdued manner that evokes a lyric and romantic feeling. He is surely as committed as his fellow "kindred spirits" but in a gentle, contemplative sort of way that lacks vibrancy but gains in its unpretentiousness and the demythicization of exaggerated emotive feelings. The poem that readily yields its meaning to an ideo-aesthetic interpretation relevant to our present effort is "For the

Decembrists," where he satirizes politicians and gives ironic accolade to the December 31, 1983 coup plotters. He sees coups as a mere change of guards and the perpetuation of the of the decadent status quo and a caricature exercise in social and political irresponsibility. "Amnestry" is another poem cast in this mode. In it, he voices out his concern for all prisoners of conscience and demands for their release. In "In Memory of Dele Giwa", he eulogizes the dead journalist and brings to the forefront the destructive elements in the society that makes it impossible for such critical and progressive human type to survive.

"Coup" (Lagos 1985), is very important as a political piece that deserves closer attention. The poem clearly states that while the "recruits" in the military bear the physical brunt of making a coup possible, the "generals" step in to give the reason for the "take-over" and take the spoils of victory:

> It is recruits who man the guns
> That keeps the passage safe
>
> All the officers need is shoot their way
> to power and provide
> The raison d'être
>
> Where the carcass is big
> Vultures are many
> The scramble for the trophy
> Ends in melee (p. 9)

The poet goes further to show that the ritual of 'taking-over' power is ceremonial and does not change anything in the society. While the "generals" continue with the army arrangement of taking the customary 21 gun salute, the material condition of the people is still precarious and woeful. He captures these ideas in the following way:

> Oh, general, climb the platform again
> Inspect the guard of honour
> Take the 21-gun salute
> From the awnings of our roof thatch
> Behind the faltering beams

Of our reed gates

We watch this annual rite
Of 'army arrangement" (p. 9)

The poet concludes that the very foundation of such an exploitative and anti-people arrangement will be destroyed by the social forces generated by neglect, poverty and hunger. Both on the military and civilian fronts, there is disenchantment and anger, which will one day be mobilized for a frontal challenge to the moribund system. He captures this in the following lines:

In the cracks of the barracks
And the tumbling roofs of the city
In the weather-worn country
Angst festers in the womb of time
And the terror of mass unrest
Stalks the outskirts of Ribadu Road!

The poem combines a lyrical narrative mode with critical social vision and prophecy. The poem also consciously aestheticizes the awaited upheaval which will transgress and subvert all the putrid dirts of the past. Atanda Ilori is, thus, clearly set to sing a lot more in the future, and as fresh songs are created, he will acquire more confidence in being a true poet of the people, and like Pablo Neruda, will say: "I made an unbreakable pledge to myself; that my people will find their voices in my songs."[17]

Adzia Ahmad's *A Shout Across the Wall*, a one hundred and fifteen page collection of seventy-one poems, does not present a unified picture of life. It is not that the poems are not successful creative reproductions of life, but that the tendencies they creatively mediate are so disparate and contradictory as to make any unified treatment of ideological and political imperatives near impossible. Poetic creations of the contemporary epoch, as against the style of proceeding generations, tend to emphasize homology of vision, continuity of idea-content and symmetry of form. Wide-ranging subjects ought not to be isolated, pocket-sized and disjointed pictures of life, but part of an organic whole through which the general thematic thrust of the entire collection finds its significance. *A Shout Across the Wall* has poems of social relevance and poems of intense personal experience. It takes every subject under the sun under its stride and probes the significance of any phenomenon-social, natural and privatist. It is precisely in the comprehensive nature of the experiences handled that the poet demonstrates his grasp and knowledge of his environment but he and the publishers demonstrate a compelling weakness by their unselective representation of his creative quests to date.

Nevertheless, there are quite a number of poems in the collection that are relevant to the subject we are discussing. Some of these are "Break Loose", "Lagos", "Ghost Riders", "IMF", "Press Freedom", "The Chimera" (SFEM/SAP) and the sequences dedicated to Thomas Sankara, the Burkinabe revolutionary leader who was assassinated on 15 October, 1987 by reactionary army officers. The poems in that sequence are "The Cadaverous Silence", "We No Longer Dance Together", "We Bivouacked under the Dreaming Star", "The Connubial Cannibal You Are" and "Your Beak in my Heart". Actually, the above poems are highly successful pieces and they work precisely because the enraged poet uses every opportunity, all available poetic devices and the enormous resources of human creative imagination to give a withering picture of decay and hopelessness. In them too, he eulogizes all positive traits and elements in society, social and human, and thereby anticipates a future of genuine progressive transformation of society. The Sankara sequences capture this sentiment in its fullness and revolutionary intensity.

"Lagos" is another very short, dramatic and sarcastic piece that summarizes the content and mode of living in an asphyxiating environment like Lagos. In the poem, the poet laments:

> EKO
> Is an echo of Hell in riot:
> An unabashed domicile of bedlam
> And breath-taking intrigue,
> A panting mass of obesity in tight pants
> Over flowing at the seams
> It is the last stop to eternity

Lagos, by extension Nigeria, in its present stage of re-colonial dependency, vulgar materialism and philistine values, is conceived as "hell in riot", a "domicile of bedlam" a "breath-taking intrigue," "a panting mass of obesity in tight pants ..." and "the last stop of eternity"; that is, the next step to damnation. "The Chimera", dedicated to SFEM/SAP, and a "song" celebrating their callous decapitation of the material well-being of the majority of Nigerians is another highly satiric poem that portrays the poet's disgust at such anti-people programmes and practices. The twin Chimera are pictured as of sprints of a "goblin" whose good quality has been taken away, "the diabolic form which this/grotesque Chimera is synthesized" and a creation so formidable that now:

> Awe struck, we grapple
> With large figures that loom
> Ominously over our horizons
> And are puzzled over the
> Hollowness of their rustling
> Sands (p. 57)

Idzia Ahmad is centrally placed in the mainstream of contemporary avant-gardist revolutionary poets and will surely make more cogent creative statements about the polity, especially, if the idea-content of his poems is projected through a logical selection of his works.

The two major deviations among the recently published poetry collections on the issue of positive concern and social commitment are Esiaba Irobi's *Cotyledons* and Afam Ake's *Stolen Moments*. This is surprising, especially in the case of

Esiaba Irobi who has been in the forefront of evolving a radical aesthetics in the Nigerian literary scene.

His plays, *The Colour of Rusting Gold* and *Hangman Also Die,* and his other collections of poetry, especially *Hand Grenades* are eloquent testimonies to his very clear and unequivocal commitment to the cause of social change and disgust at most of the foul acts of the ruling establishment. There is no doubt that the essential imperative of these works is the communication of socially-shared experiences in an ideo-aesthetic medium that is devoid of pretentiousness. His gift for the evocation of mood and atmosphere; his success in creating imagistic patterns with multivalent significations and symbolic associations; the depth of his knowledge and reading shown in the range of the experiences he creatively reproduces; and the diversity of his inter-textual references are artistic qualities and endowments unmatched by most of his contemporaries and even many of the older critical realist masters.

But what do we find when we come to *Cotyledons*? A hodgepodge mixture of myth, legend and obscure symbols parading as social poetry. No matter the depth of the personal experiences communicated and the mythic associativeness of elliptical "nature imagery" and far-flung allusions, one still expects that the balance between social vision and privatist thought could be maintained; that the tenuous link in the process of social image-making and cryptic and esoteric idiom of a rarefied mythic hue could have been preserved. Instead, a highly referential piece is divorced from its social root and left to drift along the alleyways of shamanist effusions and prophetic cant. Esiaba Irobi is easily the most gifted of the new generation of Nigerian poets and has the potential of sustainable artistic growth. One only hopes that *Cotyledons* is a poetic aberration, a centrifugal tendency in his poetic development.

The main problem of *Cotyledons* is the following unfortunate harangue in "Fresh Buds", the prefatory note to the collection:

> Myth is the language man
> Used before he invented God
> What propels a poet towards myth
> Is the impulse to understand the world
> And go beyond despair. Besides, myth
> Affords us a primitive insight into the soul
> Of man and explains in tinsel
> Metaphors, the hills and valleys of
> His undulating history including
> His contemporary volcanic experience,
> destiny.[18]

It is not even the unabashed defence of mythic structures shorn of their historicist-communal rooting, and existing autotellically outside social processes, that negates such pretension of immutability which matters here; what is of significance is this latest attempt to clothe such as esoteric garb as social commentary and political commitment and pass it off as a mythopoeic category. In charging against what he considers a single-minded ideology and open commitment to social struggle and social revolution, he points out that the crime of such culprits is that they mythify reality in their attempt to satirize and subvert the mythified reality of the uncommitted artists. The solution to this is not the unconscious mythification of the anti-mythic artists, but the deliberate mythification of reality to achieve a universal significance. This is expressed thus:

> Even now, as I write, myth explains why some cosmopolitan minds, up-rooted and alienated from their roots by their own hands, find it fashionable to rail against the mythical witchcraft of older poets. Deluded into thinking that they can impose a ghetto imagination on a people with a rich and deep-running culture, these groundlings who have no firm grounding in the nature of literature, have refused to realize that myth envelopes within its bulging muscles, the same ancient impetus that fuels our present clamour for change. This is why this

collection is called Cotyledons[19] (emphasis mine).

Cotyledon is thus the primitive plant symbol that acts as a quintessence of that original mythic knowledge and vital force that power the agony of change, and sustain its tempo. The mythic past, therefore, is the dominance of imagination, revealing the tamed present and guiding its self-search towards the catalyst of consciousness. Thus schematized and abstracted, the collection loses relevance and social value as collective artistic pieces but achieves significance and immense poetic strength and power as individual mythic structures.

The problem with Afam Akeh's *Stolen Moments* is that in the poet's attempt to apprehend the vibrant but transient "stolen moments" of existence, he neglects the larger reality from where those recorded moments are 'stolen' and abstracted. It is not that the poet is unaffected by the hustle and tedium of living in a dysfunctional social system; it is not that the harsh conditions of existence do not concern him; the fact is that the quest for private essence and personal meaning dominate his consciousness to the exclusion of public issues. The lyricism of the poems, most of which are beautifully executed is undeniable. The cluster of poignant nature imagery and profound apprehension of the minuscule of existence are remarkable, and the depth of feeling and emotion communicated worthy of any mature poet, but the fact remains that *Stolen Moments* does not quite succeed on the social level precisely because of the poet's deliberate desire to "steal" out of reality its intangible parts, as against the depiction of its dominant traits and attributes.

We can conclude that the post-civil war poets, especially in Nigeria, display a more complete awareness and appreciation of the dynamics of social development and an understanding of the inner organic law of transition of quantity into quality and quality into quality as this pertains to social-historical phenomena. They are equally more eager and willing to commit their art on the side of the majority by choosing as their subjects those issues that affect the mass of the people, and taking as their perspective the weltanschauung of the dominated classes. The revolutionary poets also, and necessarily because of the conditioning effects of re-colonization and the contradictions it engenders in all vital aspects of life, use language in a more positive, oracular, predictive and incantatory form; a gift, one can say from the prophetic idiom of the later Okigbo ("Path of Thunder"). Most of the poets of this generation are young – some are in their late twenties and early thirties – and they are understandably in a hurry, impatient to state their populist case and eager to test their poetic talent. This accounts for the lapses noticeable in their art; the attempt at misfocused myth-making; the predilection towards epiphanic delusions; and the fall, here and there, into the traps of esoteric and occult experiences, real or imagined. Beyond this however, one predicts a bright future for their art and the necessary flowering of a truly people-oriented and revolutionary ideo-aesthetic imperatives of contemporary Nigerian, nay, African poetry.

Notes and References
1. "Alter-native tradition" is a term coined by Funso Aiyejina, a dynamic Nigerian critic in an essay of the same name in The Guardian Literary series.
2. Most of these limitations have been pointed out by Chinweizu et al in their discussion on "Modern African Poetry" in Toward the Decolonization of African Literature (Enugu: Fourth Dimension, 1980).
3. Pol Ndu's poetic career was tragically act short by a fatal motor accident. Before then, he had began to establish himself as a major poetic voice, and was poised to take over from where Okigbo left off. Scholars like Romanus Eugu, Obi Maduakor and Emeka Okeke-Ezeigbo have variously commented on his art.
4. Obi Maduakor and Emeka Okeke demonstrate the

poetic efforts of these "Odunke" and "Okike" poetic voices in the early 1970s at Nsukka.
5. See D.I. Nwoga, "Modern African Poetry: The Domestication of a Tradition" in African Literature Today, No. 10, (1979).
6. Most of these poets are still in their late twenties and early thirties, and their earliest collections were published not earlier than 1987. Though newspaper articles, seminar papers and occasional reviews have appeared on their works, they are still relatively unknown to the reading public.
7. (Awka: Town Crier, 1986). Further pages references are to this edition.
8. The past songs, which are critical realist in orientation, include "Song of Lawino", "Song of Ocol", "Song of Prisoner" and "Song of Malaya", by Okot P'Bitek; "The Abandoned Hut" by John Buruga and "The Prostitute" by Okello Okuli.
9. *Resurrection* (Harmondsworth: Penguin, 1966), p. 76.
10. Quoted in Ngugi wa Thiong'o, *Writers in Politics* (London: Heinemann, 1981), p. 92.
11. See note 137 where the poem is referred to.
12. (Enugu: Delta Publishers, 1988). Further page references are to this edition.
13. *Flower Child* (Lagos: Update, 1988). Further page references are to this edition.
14. *Questions for Big Brother* (Lagos: Update, 1988). Further page references are to this edition.
15. F. Fanon, "Message to Youth of Africa." Poster quotation.
16. *Amnesty* (Lagos: Update, 1988). Further page references are to this edition.
17. Epigraph. *Songs of the Marketplace* (Ibadan: New Horn, 1983), N. p.
18. *Cotyledons* (Lagos: Update, 1988), N. p.
19. Ibid, N. p.

Part Five

THE AESTHETIC AND CULTURAL CONTEXTS OF POST-2000 NIGERIAN POETRY

This section does not pretend to be a comprehensive discussion of contemporary African, nor Nigerian poetry. Far from it. That enquiry will require a systematic study of the poetic creations of the various regions of the continent, and an analysis of the critical responses to them. What I have, rather, undertaken is a tentative probing, a modest overview of the contemporary trends in post-2000 Nigerian poetry, and also an examination of a number of maturing poetic voices of the past decade or so.

In engaging this topic, three interlocking issues stand out: the social concern of post-2000 Nigerian poetry and the expansive nature of the consciousness and the imagination of the mediating agent, which has already been treated in the introductory part of this discourse; the aesthetic dimension of the realized poetic craft, not altogether to be separated from either overly stated or concealed ideological and political imperatives of the artists; and finally, the social and cultural context of the creative process. This last issue, which naturally defines the space of artistic interrogation of objective reality, establishes the platform for the operation of ideological and aesthetic modes in a mediated form. To this extent, it becomes the point of departure in any interrogation of the poetic consciousness of the period, no matter how perfunctory such an exercise might be.

If we set our eyes fully on the self-evident assertion that no writer can write beyond the limit of his or her imagination, as perspicacious as that might be[1], the next logical issue will be an explication of the political, social, cultural and economic forces that set a limit to the consciousness of the artist. What therefore, is the composition of the reality from which writers draw their image-imperatives? Rephrased somewhat differently, what should be of interest to us here is the consideration of the social reality that exists and operates beyond the consciousness of the creative agent, the prevalent world view (weltanschauung), and the spirit that defines a writer's age (zeitgeist), all of which are embedded in the expressive processes of social interchanges and complex inter-personal and inter-group engagements.

Two fundamental conflicts have defined the postcolonial Nigerian political space in the past decade or so. The struggle for liberal capitalist democratic reforms which was given decisive impetus and push with the annulment of the June 12, 1993 presidential election[2] achieved its high water mark with the death of General Sani Abacha in June 1998 and the relatively successful transition to civil democratic governance in May, 1999.[3] Political conflicts in Nigeria, and these could be extended to other forms and dynamics of social disruption (communal, ethnic, resource based, religious, etc.) and which gained prominence partly because of the opened liberal democratic space, have not abated in the intervening years. Deep fundamental conflicts have occurred and continue to occur on three key levels: the conflict over the performance of the instruments and institutions of governance; the struggle against official corruption, graft and sleaze which has dehumanized, imbecilized and pauperized the people and has made mockery of the regime of good governance, due process, probity and accountability; and the struggle to open up the democratic space which has seen the emergence of numerous political parties and the key role civil society platforms and forces are playing in driving the democratization process[4]. We will be examining a number of the poetry collections to ascertain the degree of the poets' awareness to this shaping political dynamics (if they are interested in them, in the first place), and the pattern and mode of their artistic reflection in a number of the works.

A vital roadmap for an appreciation of the political conflict of the past decade is the congruence of oil, poverty and underdevelopment in the Niger Delta Region of Nigeria. A conflict which began as a form of passive resistance to perceived decades of injustice, neglect, underdevelopment, poverty, environmental and ecological denudation assumed, in the present millennium, a heightened degree of armed militancy, low level insurrection and elements of criminality (hostage-taking, bombing of oil platforms and flow stations, and vandalization of petroleum pipelines and other assets, etc). This interplay of aggressive dialectical forces with clear existentialist agendas weakened the national economic base with reduced oil output, and also led to the measured social, political and economic empowerment of the elite and petty-elite of the region, who are very vocal in championing such causes as "resource control", fiscal federalism revenue allocation being predicated on the principle of derivation and equal access to economic and political opportunities[5]. Again, we will be mediating in some detail the way and manner a number of the poets have brought their piercing critical ideological insight into the Niger Delta conflict through the deployment of multivalent aesthetic and stylistic resources.

On the social front, it is only natural that the "millennium poets" will devote considerable attention to the burning social issues of the time: the daily struggle for material and cultural survival, the relationship between individuals and groups as they are affected and, in turn, affect the social forces operating in their various communities, gender empowerment and equality issues, love relations, and even the admiration of the wonders of nature. What must of course, be underscored is that the social environment has been fundamentally impacted upon by the struggle for democracy and the growing and incremental consolidation of a new democratic ethic in several positive directions: free press, free speech and the liberation of creative aesthetic and artistic instincts and consciousness; a heightened sense of urgency in constructing and occupying social spaces for shared values and experiences by a multiplicity of social "voices"; and a new culture of assertiveness and confidence, spirit of daring and critical engagement with the state by individuals and groups who previously lacked the courage to express their viewpoints under the despotic, totalitarian and intolerant cloud foisted on the nation by a succession of military dictatorships between 1983 and 1998.

Of note, and this would be gleaned from a number of the poetry collections, are the persistent themes of social alienation and frustration with unbecoming social and economic conditions; generational struggle between the conservative traditionalism of the old order and the impatient modernism and even postmodernism spawned by the internet media and social network sites; struggle against loneliness, solitariness, moral ambiguities, increasingly contingent personal and communal histories, crisis in identity formation and its material and spiritual actuation and social reclusion which urban existence sometimes spawns; and most importantly, the different contexts of feminist consciousness and social agitation powered by education, economic self-reliance and inter-cultural exposure.

Ify Agwu's *Amidst the Blooming Tempest*[6] is a good example of those poetic works that bestride the threshold of social didacticism and strident criticism of certain unbecoming oddities that define the Nigerian social and political landscape. Ify Agwu's aesthetic consciousness and artistry is still maturing, with hopefully a fuller application of the variegated literary resources that will balance his thematic visions, aesthetic delivery and ideological clarity. In "Let Them Know", for example, he is insistent on the necessity of a new, peaceful world order that can only come about when "no man shall raise a sword/against his brother". Some other poems in the collection also capture, in graphic detail, the dire consequences of ethnic and communal strife, a sordid reality that Nigerians are daily grappling with given the recurring barbarous blood-letting in the Benue Valley states, particularly Plateau, Benue, Taraba and Nasarawa States and the new terrorist and extremist insurgencies indicated with the spate of bomb blasts across the country[7]. His satiric mode of delivery is very effective in his trenchant opposition to the misery, human losses and social and economic dislocations that necessarily trail bloody communal conflict and sectarian violence.

Jude C. Ogu's *The Trial of Wazobia,*[8] a title that echoes Ali Mazrui's *The Trial of Christopher Okigbo,* combines both the dramatic resource of theatre (a mock trial) with symbolic association of meaning, "time and results", to create a world of lost promises and possibilities and unrealized hopes and aspirations. The main poem in the collection, "Wazobia" (an acronym derived from the languages of Nigeria's major ethnic groups), deals with the perennial issue of Africa's wasted opportunities and aborted historical promises. The poet holds African postcolonial leaders squarely responsible for the parlous state of affairs in the continent and, deploying the aesthetic devices of rhetoric and polemics, passes a vote of no confidence on a visionless group of self-seeking and self-serving rulers who remain clueless about the challenges that confront the continent.

Segi Adigun has three collections of poetry to his credit (*Kalakiri: Song of Many Colours,* 2004; *Band on the Shore,* 2005; and *Prayer for Mwalimu*[10]). Of these, the last collection is the most political, in which he adeptly and boldly delivers a clarion call for positive action by the people in order to install good leaders who will rescue a nation on the throes of despair. For the poet, Nigeria is a nation adrift, floundering in the valley of despair, disillusionment, underdevelopment and hopelessness, without any sustainable anchor. The poet's tone is shrill, elegiac and incantatory in turns, reflecting different patterns of changing moods, and illustrating also his combativeness, sense of despair and angst, especially with the unfettered reign of selfishness which the hard times have spawned. There is also a clear sign that the poet is intent on developing his aesthetic craft through the utilization of the Eliotian "objective correlative" artistic idiom in the poem "Pompholyx", a pseudonymic capturing of chicken pox, as well as the poet's metaphor that only people who care and love one another can overcome the ravages of such social maladies, and work towards common social, economic, cultural and political goals and aspirations.

If there is any collection of poems that best illustrates our earlier comment on contemporary Nigerian poets broaching issues of wide social concerns, it must be Mabel Evierhoma's *A song as I Am and Other poems*.[11] The collection could be best described as a miscellany of poems that touches on various social themes: self confidence, wifehood, nostalgic love, innovation and creativity, and industry and hard work. Just as *Out of Hiding*, her earlier work, the "songs" are carefully crafted as didactic artistic pieces that are meant to teach and edify, and also as a handy tool in understanding life and its multiform complexities. Worthy of attention with regard to her poetic craft is that, in spite of the feminist tinge of some of the poems, the poet successfully adopts an ambivalent posture that reinforces a deep sensitivity to the subjects being treated. This is most noticeable in the poems dealing with womanhood, especially "Nuptial Counsel", in which a girl-child boldly confronts her mother's lesson on absolute obedience in wifehood. By balancing the conventional with the radical, the traditional with the innovative, the poet presents an image of a society in flux and transition, and capable of summoning the wisdom of years gone by to aid the self-assertive quest of contemporary individuals.

Both Humphrey Onyima and Denja Abdullahi are to be counted among the emerging voices in the Nigerian poetic scene. While Onyima espouses a youthful brand of political militancy against the recurring decimals of corruption, governmental ineptitude and general societal drift, and calls for radical social and political transformation of the polity, Abdullahi expresses his aesthetic consciousness in the complex nuances of nature, cultural landmarks and beautiful landscapes. Onyima's *Gunshots*[12] is a form of literary handgrenade with which the poet is intent on exploding the rot in society. Interspaced with essays, quotations from great leaders; and deploying the artistic resources of graphic imagery, parallelisms, rhetorical devices, metaphoric sequences of poignantly versified narratives, the collection displays a mind in a hurry to change society, and a stubborn hope that out of the ashes of the present day decay will emerge a future defined by liberty, freedom and social justice.

Denja Abdullahi's *Abuja Nunyi* [13] is however, a different kind of work altogether. It can best be described as "tour poetry"; a poeticization of tourist attractions, nature imagery and landscapes in Nigeria's capital city and beyond. Poems like "Gbagji", "Dances" and "Giri Porters" will serve as a good guide to tourists who want to seek out the aesthetic endowments of the city, especially in an elegant, poetic form. Possibly one of the few exceptions to this type of poetry is "To the First Poet Laureate", a tribute to Mamman Vatsa, a soldier-poet who was implicated in a 1986 coup d'état and was subsequently executed. In the poem, the poet creatively underscores the pervasive culture of impunity and intolerance which has dogged the Nigerian political environment for a long time.

Worth mentioning also here is Enobong Uwemedimo's

Reminiscences which adorns both a celebratory and chastising mood at the same time. In the collection, the poet celebrates crops like cassava, kola nut and corn. Innovative endeavours are praised but the sense of disconnection, alienation and social and ethical disorders found in Nigerian cities receive severe critical censure. Stylistically, the poet deploys the resources of Pidgin English, dialogue and code mixing and switching to deepen poetic centers of consciousness. Relatedly, lyrical devices provide the humorous idiom which disguises and often time, conceals the tragic note that skirts most of the poems in the collection.

One positive note in contemporary Nigerian poetry is the persistence of established poetic voices whose poetic craft dates two decades or more. In responding to the changed and changing times, these mature poets either reinforce their noted aesthetic idiosyncrasies or even add more artistic devices to their already extensive creative repertoire. J.P. Clark-Bekederemo and Niyi Osundare are worthy of specific mention here. These two poets need no introduction though J.P. Clark is somewhat noted more for his contributions to the growth and development of African drama than for his poetic craft, in spite of the tremendous success of *Casualties* and his other collected works of poetry.[17] The same could be said of Niyi Osundare who many adjudge to be a worthy successor to the later Chris Okigbo and Okot P'Bitek, and considered to be arguably Africa's greatest living poet.[18]

J.P. Clark's *Mandela and Other Poems* is a reworking of the 1988 premier edition as the collection, with added socio-political motifs pervading its poetic landscape. The core poem, "Mandela" ruminates on the predicament of the iconic leader at the time he was a prisoner in Robben Island for his anti-apartheid agitation:

> How does the old man spend his day?
> In the cage...
> Away from his wife,
> Away from life

Through such introspective thought and rhetorical questioning, the poet not only captures the state of alienation and solitude by a specific individual but also underlines the theme of suffering, humiliation and torture through associative symbolic devices. The poet's ideo-aesthetic perspective is thus piercingly profound in locating the culture of impunity, silence and fear which is also a Nigerian postcolonial political phenomenon.

Niyi Osundare expresses the prevalent contemporary Nigerian mood in his *The Word is an Egg*, a collection in which the spoken word assumes a life of its own and is imbued with superlative and supernatural force: it can build as it can destroy being the originator of all essences:

> In the beginning was not the word
> In the word was the beginning (10)

In this context, the poet makes reference to the role of honest communication and dialogue in dousing political and social tension, and provides poetic insight on how to sustain democracy in the new millennium. For example, the curious trickish word-plays: "Build now /gulf after" is an admonition to politicians whose atavistic mindset is couched on the sham philosophy of seeing elections as a do or die affair.

In addition, poems like "I Have Learnt Pregnant Word", provides concrete proof of the latent power in the word – "every verb stings like a bee" (44), thus calling attention to great personages who were destroyed by mere utterance:

> Some words burn
> I look once again
> At the emperor's statue (45)

By blending the social and the ritual, the mythic and the religious, in the ever-widening context of social and political engagement, Osundare produces yet another masterly creative work that goes a long way in reinforcing his towering stature in African literature.

What we will do at this stage is to examine both the broad

and specific ideo-aesthetic concerns of post-2000 Nigerian poetry by taking a close analytic look at two collections of poetry: K.K. Iloduba's *In the Arms of Misery* and Angela Awosu's *Waking Dreams*.[19] *In the Arms of Misery* could be thematically read at various though inter-connected levels: as the poeticization of the mood of denial and deprivation in the oil-rich but developmentally backward, poverty- ridden and ecologically denuded Niger Delta Region of Nigeria ("Sepulcher", p. 22, "Misery I" and II, pp16,28); as an imaginative apprehension of the raging storm of disquiet and restlessness in the region ("Time Lapse", p.14, and "The Visitor" p.15); as a spasmodic yearning for "resource control" which is posited as an alternative to the force of political autonomy and self-determination conditioned by a centrifugal passion ("Destiny", p.33); and finally, as an account of the sense of alienation and disillusionment with the Nigerian Federation by people who feel completely abandoned and neglected ("New Nigeria", p. 49, "Mr. President", p. 49 , and "False B", p. 19).

In the Arms of Misery is rich in aesthetic devices and stylistic features. One readily underscores the poet's effort to match subject-matter with style, in order to achieve unity between theme and form. The story of the Niger Delta is the story of pain, loss, dislocation – social, economic and psychological; and neglect, poverty and ecological and environmental damage. But it is also the story of struggle, conflict, anger, agitation and the restless quest for various forms of social, economic and political amelioration. These contrasting image-imperatives are driven home forcefully with multivalent aesthetic resources that leave no one in doubt about the depth of the poet's passion and commitment to the issues he raises.

For instance, we are inescapably drawn to the fact that he balances mood and feeling in some of the poems with the deployment of searing, scorching, fiery and rhetorical devices. This could be seen in "Blood and Sands" (18); "The Voice" (38); and "The Rhythm" (20). Furthermore, we detect a rhythmic flow that appropriately reflects a feeling of anxiety, insecurity and restlessness, making virtually all the poems racy, harried and flighty in nature. Equally so, as is to be expected, the diction in a number of the poems is grisly and incendiary, and overly sentimental with reference to the volatile dynamics of oil politics in the region. Examples of this are to be seen in "Time Lapse" (15); "Blood and Sands" (18); and "The Rhythm" (22).

Furthermore, the poet utilizes a serendipitic, locational sensibility in a number of the poems ("Here Where Oil Greases" (13); "Over These Mournful Skies" (16); and "In This Place" which all refer to the region, as well as contrasting phenomenological symbols and images ("a once lush vineyard now decimated" (17); "a militarized land of misery" (15); a "sepulcher" (23); "a land marked by agony" (23); "a chamber of doom" (24); and a "gale of desolation" (21).

Apart from the collection's multi-layered levels of meaning and symbolic implicatur, most of the poems in it are characterized by the poet's acute awareness of Africa's rich poetic tradition and debt to the continent's finest poetic minds. He thus uses inter-textual references and healthy borrowings to embolden and ennoble his themes and poetic vision. Examples of these are to be seen in a reference to Lord Byron's poem about Joan of Arc: "How will freedom lift up her voice? / When will the captive's cry be attended to?" (13). There is also reference to J.P. Clark's poem "Ibadan", in which Ogoniland is described as:

> A once lush vineyard
> New battered,
> Shattered and scattered

From David Diop also comes the following borrowing:

> If we seek to have hope.....
> What tale would we tell?
> What door would dare....?
> What smell would.......? (16, 27)

Iloduba's socio-aesthetic vision is realized through a persuasive combination of political consciousness and creative and artistic imagination. His poetic craft seems to have been galvanized towards addressing the aspirations of the Niger Delta communities. He achieves this by utilizing a polemical device that is intense as could be seen in "Waking the Dead" (58); by being unabashedly political:

> *They kill all our nature and defile our rivers"*
> *("Waking the Dead" (51) and How have you changed"*
> *How have your gushes become curses ("Oil" 11, 47)*
>
> *And through the power of prophecy:*
> *Beneath this......*
> *Lies a swift-scented heaven*
> *("Heaven in Sight", 58).*

Verbal militancy also aids the realization of the poet's objective intention as demonstrated in "We jolt the hills with our shout/And the valleys will cry out" ("Destiny" 11, 37)

Finally, virtually all the poems are engaged and committed.

Passionate engagement and commitment thus becomes a weapon of poetic combat as seen in the poem, "Mr. President":

> *Does not your conscience*
>   *nag?*
> *These hungry look that*
>   *swell*
> *The band of unhappy*
>   *masses*
> *These battered and scattered*
>   *folks (49)*

In Arms of Misery is properly situated at the juncture where politics marries art in a harmonious union. It extends the possibility of history and the dialectics of struggle creatively mediated and imaginatively rendered. And in so doing, it echoes the tragedies and the triumphs, the travails and the obstinate hopes of the Niger Delta people, a landscape and mindscape that was immortalized by Ken Saro-Wiwa in the *Forest of Flowers*:

> Now and again we would drive past
> A gas flame reminding us that this
> Was an oil-bearing country and that from the
> Bowels of this land came the much-sought
> After liquid which fuelled the wheels of
> Modern civilization.[20]

It will be safe to say that *In the Arms of Misery* continues the tradition of postcolonial African writing that shows strong preoccupation with socio-political matters as against the deep and profound creative analysis, exploration and interpretation of individual conduct and motivations, passions and even psychic conditioning.

K.K. Iloduba, on his part, emerges as the archetypal emergent African poet passionate about the forces and processes that shape his environment, and is completely engaged with and committed to ameliorating them. The limits set to his artistic vision and poetic repertoire are many, yet are over-compensated by his ideo-political clarity of perspective and a guileless and almost single-minded ownership and authentication of the struggle of all oppressed peoples.

When we come to Angela Awosu's *Waking Dreams*,[21] a totally different picture emerges. The collection is characterized by thematic unity and could be read at various levels. We detect now the conflict between patriarchal traditionalist ethos which limits women's self-assertive and affirmative propensities and desires and the currents of modernism which extend the frontiers of possibilities. There is also the theme of identity-search, an agonizing process of self-examination and self-mastery from the prison of self-insecurity to the sure platform of self-liberation. Beyond these two grand thematic trajectories are also to be underscored the deep exploration of human emotions and human psychology: self-doubt and self-rejection, sense of anguish and frustration, an inscrutable mindscape that serves as a canvas for life's challenges and uncertainties, unrequited love and mental handicap, but above all, an abiding faith in humanism and love, and of the indestructible human spirit that triumphs over existential oddities and travails.

We will now proceed to situate some of these thematic assertions through a close reading of the text. What jumps out forcefully is the traditional definition of complete womanhood in Africa – a husband, a child and a home – and the cultural incompleteness of femininity that disavows these values. The words of a traditional Swahili poem speak powerfully of this:

> Give me the minstrel seat......
> Let me ask why women refuse to marry?
> Woman cannot exist except by man
> A woman is she who has a husband...
> ...rich man and poor man.......
> Join hands across the shroud.

The importance of this is that in spite of the lacerations by Western post-modernist cultural consciousness on African traditional cultural imperatives, the African society loathes, ridicules and shames an unmarried woman in spite of her social, economic and political standing in society. Awosu's poems spring from deep concerns about this cultural entrapment, an emotional journey that operates at the twilight zone between reality and consciousness; between a burdensome cultural heritage and the need for catharsis and self-release; and between an awareness of self-possibilities and the limits set by cultural, social and moral conventions.

This sense of cultural entrapment engenders multiple emotional responses as is demonstrated by the following:

Emotional and physical crisis is indicated in the "chain" (7); and seclusion, isolation, and even self-hibernation are seen in "I am an island unto myself/ carry my crosses/ my self-shift" in "An Island" (8); self-dejection and low self-esteem:

> For all I care
> I may be in the cloud
> Or alien in the mood
> I may be suspended
> in the air
> May be said.... ("For All I Care", (9)

A haunting spectre of frustration, hysteria, nightmare, a nebulous mindscape and loss pervade the entire poetic atmosphere; these are to be seen in the following:

> I am in the wild forest
> Doing a dance with snakes
>
> Drinking toxins ("Mood",(4))
> We live to survive
> We put God aside and plunged
>   Bigger sins
> ...new costumes harsher to
>   Behold
> We have become hysterical,
> The demin's surrogates
> The cracks are visible in the
>   Great new sins....
> ...the rainbow promise is
>   Dead, killed
> We have doomed ourselves.....
> Marriage proposal wasted through
>   Indecision....
> Cupid, poised with his bow
> Waited to shoot his arrow
> But I, afraid to plunge
>   ("Yes and No", 30)
> I see you...
> I hear you...
> I breathe you...

> *I hearken ...*
> *I can still see you winking*
> *At me ("Ubiquitous", 31)*
> *Malumfashi, don't take flight now*
> *My fixation is genuine*
> *("Malumfashi", 35)*

Awosu's social vision is not all clothed with the garb of pain and despair. We have already indicated the possibility of personal, social and cultural reconciliation in the preceding discussion. The motif of identity-search and self-discovery is an unending human enterprise, yet the clouds can sometimes lift up, and the hidden truth of near and distant selves are instantly revealed. We see this in the poem, "Freedom":

> *I break my madness*
> *Fight my pains*
> *Walk in the sun*
> *I become a flood of light (47)*

For the poet persona, therefore, the question the African woman has to ponder about is the proper location of those "seeds of truth" that make a woman a woman.

Awosu deploys an impressive array of stylistic resources to realize her poetic vision. For a start, most of the poems employ the autobiographical identification mode of "I", "We" and "Us" to capture vividly and also own the painful life-situations imaginatively recreated. The stream of consciousness technique, very popular in prose fiction and post-modernist literature in general, features prominently as a mean of objectifying the nuances of existence implanted in the poet's conscious mind. This allows the poet to project a continuous stream and succession of thoughts, emotions and feelings, both vague and well defined, that form the pre-Freudian and post-Freudian experiences captured in the poems.

Worthy of mention also is her sparse use of verse, which sometimes dwindles into nothingness, as demonstrated in "Chain" and "Ubiquitous". Sparseness of verse and its gradual miniaturization is indicative of the "littleness" of the persona and her descent into a state of "nothingness" or non-being, a tragic human state that is culturally conditioned. Added to this is Awosu's allusive and intertextural cross references, showing her wide reading and debt to great poets like Lord Byron, Percy Bessye Shelley and William Blake:

> I see Byron roaming the
> Wilds of Greece
> Shelley in voyage....
> Blake among lamb...
>   ("Mood", 14)

These allusions help to evoke appropriate mood and feeling of a mind encased in a trapped body.

Awosu's debt to Okigbo is also self-evident. The invocation of Okigbo's spirit by means of a sinewy idiom that re-enacts the late poet's rainbow world renders her journey of search motif in authentic terms. This is vividly captured in "Strange" through the distances-song sequence and in "Triumphant Entry" in the Heaven's Gate, Thunder and Rain sequences. However, the climatic end of Okigbo's oracular voice is counterbalanced by Awosu's comatose imagery, of quietide and stillness, a force that clothes her art with a tragic aura.

Waking Dreams shows great artistic promise and is written by an artist who is still refining her vision and firming up her poetic craft. It not only demonstrates an organic and unified poetic movement that accommodates the complex structuring of human cosmological paradigms and sensibilities – terrestrial and extra-terrestrial, subconscious and conscious awareness of being – all tissues of cultural conditioning and reality that illuminate the known and hidden universe. The collection captures the four dimensions of life in their individuality and totality, through a deft probing of human responses to both declared and hidden cultural impulses, and in so doing successfully balances the social and moral concerns of art with its fidelity as an aesthetic category without disabling the authenticity of the other.

Post-2000 Nigerian poetry is a consequence of a complex medley of cultural, aesthetic and political forces underpinned by postcolonialist institutional platforms at their most traumatic phase of development: their traumas and stresses; contradictions and disunities; and integral group identities and individual narratives powered by the emblem of discontents. Whether they are good poetic creations (and there are glaring aesthetic evidences that some of the collections I have examined are mostly of a mediocre mode), is not the point being stressed. At issue, is the interrogation of a generational poetic momentum sustained by a heightened degree of literary exuberance and imperative, and directed at one clear signpost at the threshold of a dawning every one of them can predict: to mediate the shapes, contours and spiritual nuances that define a milieu, to summon and harness reality in the search of individual and collectives voices, and in the best Aristotelian paradigm of catharsis, to exorcise the demons of alienation, turbulence and existential terror that negate humanity's essence in an era of unbelief and faithlessness.

There is no doubt that postcolonial literary strategists have focused their theoretical and critical constructs in the direction of new Nigerian poetry, partly in the justification of the requirement for academic and scholarly advancement and promotion, but also partly as a form of passionate social engagement that sees in the poetic works under consideration, the parable of resistance to social nihilism, spiritual ataraxia and political apostasy of a generation that seems to have lost its way. My intention in placing on record this rash of critical commentaries, has very little to do with a close examination of the postcolonialist pet terms: alterity, hybridity and self and the other (within and outside a defined cultural mainstream), transculturation, transnationalism and translocation; terms that are, more often than not, forms of ideological concealment, denial and rationalization. Most tragically, too, these terms are the re-situations and re-insertions of the discursive modes of obscurantist postmodernist, poststructuralist and deconstructionist theoretic exertions into postcolonial intellectual spaces, both in the deterritorialized diasporic cultural havens and in the postcolonial academic margins.

My task is a modest one: to examine a number of the critical observations on contemporary Nigerian poetry with the hope that the poems I have studied could be better placed in their social, cultural and aesthetic context, even when some of them fail as exemplary poetic creations. To achieve this, I summon the wisdom of Niyi Osundare's interview with *Sahara Reporters* on a broad range of issues dealing with Nigerian literature, canonization and critical and aesthetic philosophy of the arts. Regarding the creative craft of the younger generation of Nigerian literary artists, Osundare observes thus:

> What we have is a platter of contradictions. On the one hand, we have a lot of enthusiasm, especially from the younger writers or those coming to the literary scene for the first time ...... Books are being published, especially those on poetry. And I think that the stakes are disproportionately in favour of poetry. The way things are at the moment, It appears that for every five books of poetry you publish, you probably get a book of prose. And for every 10 books of poetry published, there is one book of drama.[23]

In the same interview, Osundare dismisses the literary and aesthetic value of a great number of those works, an issue that also occupies significant space in Amanze Akpuda's "A Dream Beyond the Pyramids". In what I consider a seminal discourse on the evolution of Nigerian literature from 1986 to the late 1990s, dealing as it does with the issues of history, canonization, literary trends and movements, internecine creative and critical battles among dominant literary figures, and the problematic question of the evaluation of literary works for prize awards, all placed in the context of the metaphors of ferment, harvest, bazaar and carnival, Akpuda makes the following comments:

> Among such critics who have broached the problems of poeticity or or its absence in new Nigerian poetry are Olu Oguibe, Chinweizu, Frank Uche Mowah, John Otu, Femi Osofisan, Obi Nwakanma,... Olu Oguibe is probably the first major Nigerian literary critic to voice his distaste for the low quality work produced by writers of his generation... {He} reveals the depth to which poetry in Nigerian has sunk in recent years: a low level accomplishment in the art and craft, no critical attention whatever...[24]

Akpuda also foregrounds the scathing critique of Chinweizu in his article "20th Century African Literature: Feast and Famine" regarding the retarded creative imagination of the emergent breed of writers in Nigeria and elsewhere and Tanure Ojaide's extremist postulation "that there is nothing like new Nigerian poetry and that the writers so identified are essentially copycat authors always desperate to search for the next available publisher to "publish" their works".[25] Nevertheless, "A Dream Beyond Pyramids" is rich in locating the forces that shape the creative imagination and social consciousness of the younger generation of literary artists, the role of creative writing courses and classes in molding and expanding creative excursions and technical ability, and the salutary role of a thriving publishing industry in giving voice to hidden wisdom.[26]

Going back to Osundare's apparently dismissive though apt observation about the dominant place poetry occupies in the creative pursuits of the younger generation of Nigerian writers, Oyeniyi Okunoye in "Writing Resistance: Dissidence and Visions of Healing in Nigerian Poetry of the Military Era" avers as follows:

> Anyone familiar with the growth of Nigerian literature after the civil war will have no difficulty appreciating why the genre of poetry dominated Nigerian writing, especially from the mid-1980s to the late 1990s. In a sense, the prevailing political climate in the country created the atmosphere for it to thrive. Proof that Nigerian poetry has been very dynamic is that it has drawn on a variety of experiences.[27]

Okunoye goes on to list those significantly impactful experiences as the political crisis of the 1960s, the civil war of 1967-970 and the prolonged period of military misrulership of Nigeria: 1966-79, 1983-1999 (28). As has already been observed, this dominance of poetry has persisted into the first and second decades of the 21st century, drawing as it does new national traumas and social, political and economic challenges as Nigeria negotiates haunting cross-roads of implacable dilemmas in its march towards liberal capitalist democratization process and social transformation.

Another point worth noting in Okunoye's analysis is the pervasive presence of militant school of Nigerian poetry, consequent upon the activism and martyrdom of Ken Saro-Wiwa, and the wider struggle for social amelioration, economic empowerment and political mainstreaming in the Niger Delta Region; and issues which I dealt with in some length in K.K. Iloduba's *In the Arm of Misery*. Okunoye stresses this point thus:

> The killing of Ken Saro Wiwa along with other Ogoni activists inspired the third major trend in Nigerian poetry of the 1990s. Apart from being imaginatively recreated events in Nigerian poetry within the decade, it has inspired the flowering of a trans-ethnic tradition of resistance poetry in the Niger Delta region. The tradition thrives on shared sensed of violation and marginal consciousness...Ojaide's *Delta Blues and Home Songs (1997)*, Adiyi Bestman's *Textures*

of Dawn (1998) and Ogaga Ifowodo's *The Oil Lamp* (2005) operate within this tradition.[29]

Okunoye's concluding remarks with regard to the ideo-aesthetic texture of the new Nigerian poetry; a tradition that is sustained up to the present is very succinct. He juxtaposes the implications of social and political atavism with the liberationist paradigm of hope and ideology of societal renewal thus:

> The fact that the poet went beyond envisioning an end to the chaotic state of affairs to imagining a new dawn for their land indicates that they saw the vision of change as the only viable alternative to despairing. They therefore invest images of renewal, rebirth and fulfillment in a future that holds prospects of recovery and the fruition of their dreams for Nigeria.[30]

Okunoye wrote with regard to the poets of the 1980s and 1990s. I have no doubt that he more than anticipates the consciousness of the poets of the 21st century, whose search for the hidden portals of Nigerian humanity is fraught with traumas and setbacks as powerful and poignant as the challenges faced by their poetic fore-runners.

Evidence abounds about the dominance of the poetic genre in contemporary Nigerian literary craft. Individual collections and published anthologies attest to the vitality of this enduring tradition, from the sustained output of the established poetic voices to the fledgling creative imagination of the enterprising, exuberant but uncertain poetic consciousness of the younger breed of writers; and from the bursting buds of creative ferment in literary taverns, cafes and festivals, some of which have been put out in the public domain in published form, to the increasing recognition of the creative enterprise of female poets who are steadily finding their voice and mastering their vision and craft.

For example, between 1999 and 2010, Niyi Osundare and

Tanure Ojaide, arguably Nigeria's best two poets of the Second Generation writers, have published the following collections of poetry, drama and critical studies: Niyi Osundare: *The Word is an Egg* (Ibadan: Kraft Books, 2000); *Pages From the Book of the Sun: New and Selected Poems* (Trenton, NJ: African World Press, 2002); *Thread in the Loom*: Essays on African Literature and Culture (Trenton, NJ: African World Press, 2002); and *The State Visit* (a play)(Ibadan: Kraft books, 2002.[31] And from Tanure Ojaide: *When it No Longer Matters Where You Live (1999); Invoking the Warrior Spirit: New Selected Poems(1999); In the Kingdom of Songs: Poems 1995-2000 (2002); I want to Dance and other Poems (2003); In the House of Words (2006); The Tale of the Harmattan (2007); and Waiting for the Hatching of a Cockerel (2008)*.[32]

Two critical commentaries, among numerous others, that shed light on Osundare's adroit application of Yoruba proverbial and idiomatic usages and sometimes cryptic linguistics pattern and mode of signification in handling social and political satire are Emmanuel Folorunso Taiwo's "A Reading of Yoruba Proverbial as Socio-Political Satire in Osundare's *Waiting Laughters"*[33] and Uzoechi Nwagbara's engaging reading of Ojaide's *When it longer Matters Where You Live* as a postcolonialist interrogation of the motifs and metathematics of exile, transnationalism and translocational discontents.[34]

Apart from the following anthology of poems: *A Volcano of Voices* (1999); *Uncle Bola's Promise* (2003); *Confluence Blues* (2004); *Abuja Acolytes*(2000); *Five Hundred Nigerian Poets* (2005); *Camouflage* (2006); *Pyramids* (2008); and *Fire Flies* (2009) all of which are designed to create space and visibility, and give public voice to the under-represented and least exposed emergent poets, there is the noted sustained research effort to mainstream female Nigerian poets in this evolving poetic tradition. Worthy of mention here are Aderemi Raji-Oyelade's "Notes Towards the Bibliography of Nigerian Women Poetry (1985-2006)"[35] and Ismail Bala's

"Women Poetry from Northern Nigeria: A Bibliographic Note."[36]

Some critical attention has been targeted at the resistance poetry from Nigeria's Niger Delta Religion,[37] the dominant thematic focus of Iloduba's *In the Arm of Misery*. This is not surprising given that the social complexes and traumas, identity related issues, and significations of political contradictions in the context of the centre-margin dialectic that define the postcolonial Nigerian State are located in the region's different structures and forms of narratives.

Yet, the broad field of contemporary Nigerian poetry has continued to attract multivalent critical exposure. One such very recent research effort is Sule E. Egya's "Art and Courage: A Critical Survey of Recent Nigerian Poetry in English".[38] Another is S.S. Olaoluwa's "African Poetry and the Politics of Exile: A Critical Survey"[39] which made some use of the first edition of the current work in its ambitious location of the poetics of disconnectedness, moral ambiguities and cultural discontinuities in transmigratory African literary experience. But by far, two of the most extensive examinations of New Nigerian Poetry are Chin Ce's "A Dance of the Ether: Four Decades of African Poetry in English" and GMT Emezue's "History, Vision and Craft in New Nigerian Poetry". Concerning the Third Generation of African Poets, Chin Ce declares thus:

> The flame now burns in the hands of drummers strumming angry notes for the rude shocks that have rattled the African land and people from within... Some of these younger poets are set to inscribe forever the dreams, sentiments and energies of their history with a trenchant fortitude that has hardly been witnessed in preceding periods.[40]

Even more than Chin Ce, Emezue locates the socio-aesthetic trajectories of the new generation poets of the 1980s and 1990s in a manner that resonates deeply and profoundly with the poetic craft of the post-2000 poetic voices, as a reading of the earlier part of his discourse would have shown:

> These new brands of mournful poetry are expressed in voices not alien to their surrounding despite the several occurrence of modern styles. Of interest in this study is the poetic threnodies which style of rendition is drawn from spheres of human endeavour. It could be the loss sustained from betrayal of trust, disappointment in relationships, denial and deprivation of rights and the sense of atrophy experienced from injured visions.[41]

Continuing, Emezue argues that:

> Wherever a poet utilizes *the threnodic voice in* his poetry, such poems differ in terms of sentiment. Nigerian poets are thence caught expressing despair, gloom, hopelessness, melancholy, despondency, disencouragement, bitterness, desperation, and shock. These feelings are also expressed through a language of ire, anger, passion, fiery, exasperation, trepidation, cynicism, bitterness, sarcasm, ridicule, derision, irony, grief, distress, misery, woe and anguish.[42]

What, of course, should be added is that the emotions and passions detailed above are interconnected tissues of shared values and experiences, and a shared belief that out of the welter of social disconnections, dislocations and cultural dilemmas and incompleteness the struggle for re-humanization of individuals and entities is an attainable ideal. This is the message of Nigerian poets, their sense of social engagement and creative enterprise. However, Emezue's comment that "in spite of the mass of voices... only a few of these layers of poetic expression yield their underlying message"[43] is a dire challenge facing all followers of the poetic muse, all the bards waiting in the wings to find and use their voice, for as Senator Ihenyen muses in

"Contemporary Nigerian Poetry – Which Way?" that even though poetic, consciousness, vision and artistic direction is very pervasive in Nigeria, poets in the making must exercise extra caution and avoid haste in their creative quest.[44]

Conclusion

Every generation draws its breath from the sounds, smells and sights that surround it; and from the inscrutable nuances that its age incarnates. Whether in the context of culture and its material expositions, and those other image-imperatives that seek for significations outside the wellspring of materiality, the breath of a generation is the living spirit of culture, and the consciousness of it. In politics, this breath wears a dissonant aura, from the cultural and identity disconnects, ambiguities and discontinuities foisted on the African subalterns by colonialism, to the exaggerated claims of Western liberal democracy with its transformative postmodernist end of history clap trap in the postcolonial margins. There is no doubt that the invasion of African postcolonial spaces by the raging currents of late, postmodern capitalism is inherently insufficient, if not, out rightly impotent in constructing a platform for the contestation of ideas and the realization of visions- personal and collective. Yet, this logic of ideological determinations through denial readily advertises its insolent insistence that the ascendancy of a one-way translocational and transnational globalist ideology will heal all of the wounds of misgovernance, mass pauperization and imbelicization, not to say, the sheer destruction of a nation's institutions and structures from where procreative social processes emanate.

There is yet the third generational breath that lies at the crossroads of various cultures; the cultural imaginings of people as themselves, the burden of postcoloniality, and the double tragedy of postmodernism. This is the breath of daily want and living, of loving and dying, of smelling defeat and experiencing triumphs in the little things that matter. Yet, there is a hidden thread, an umbilicus that connects the navel of the present to the past of knowing, of becoming. It is this navel of life as people know it that post-modernist scholarship and its various layered, narcissistic tributaries want to sever.

The experiences that enrich the poetic visions of the poets I have examined, even when they fail to make the mark, are not reader-induced meanings emanating out of self-concealing narratives nor the disjointed and nihilistic cultural subjectivities incubated in the laboratories of theory. Reading the poems is to draw breath from objective fact and objective life and to situate the pains of our contemporary condition on the material parameters set by an unjust social system and grossly unequal material relations of production and power – cultural and political. It is also to declare with clarity, if not audacity, that the journey of life is an infinite progression of existence and reality, and the ideas that nourish them. Crucially so, it is a journey towards the mass mobilization of our people with the weapon of truth, knowledge and passion for the endless confrontation against dehumanization – a necessary condition for the freeing of the human spirit, the affirmation of human possibility and the certainty of human transformation. This constitutes the integral message from our poets, a world apart from the anemic systematization and academicization of knowledge, often times belched out for its own obscurantist sake.

Notes and References
1. Georg Lukacs (*The Historical Novel, History and Class Consciousness, The Meaning of Contemporary Realism, Studies in European Realism,* etc) posits that in spite of the broad and perspicacious range of a writer's imagination, he can neither organize nor mediate reality beyond the limit set by his consciousness. Consciousness, on its part, is mainly a derivative of material life not in a mechanical one-on-one correspondence but in a dialectal cause-and-effect unity,

as Eagles once observed. The materialist reading of history and culture establishes a compass of coherence and progression in the relationship between dominant and dominated ideological material forces that readily denies and negates the postmodernist nihilistic, subjectivist, anarchic and incoherent apprehension of reality as self-canceling reader-induced narratives.

2. On 24th June, 1993, the military regime of General Ibrahim Babangida annulled the result of the June 12, 1993 Presidential election which was won by the late Chief M.K.O. Abiola. This action unleashed disruptive and centrifugal social and political forces that threatened Nigeria's unity and corporate existence. The post-annulment political period witnessed the toppling of the interim government led by Chief Ernest Shonekan by General Abacha on 17th November, 1993, who governed in a repressive, totalitarian and despotic manner until his death in June 1998. Opposed to the military dictatorships of the time were wide-ranging platforms of pro-democracy, human rights and labour activists whose struggles eventually ended military rule on 29th May, 1999.

3. As indicated above, the death of General Sani Abacha and the emergence of Gen. Abdulsalami Abubakar as Nigeria's Head of State opened the political space, liberalized political participation and oversaw the transition to civil democratic rule that began on 29th May, 1999 under a multi-party presidential constitutional arrangement.

4. Apart from the fact that the constitution review and amendment process only occurred in 2010, between 1999 and 2011 several attempts have been made to expand the regime, scope and horizon of good governance, accountability and the "war" against corruption, graft and sleaze through the establishment of the Economic and Financial Crimes Commission (EFCC) and the Independent Corrupt Practices

Commission (ICPC) by Acts of Parliament. The period also witnessed the burgeoning of democracy-building and election-reform civil society platforms like the Transition Monitoring Group(TMG) and the Alliance for Credible Elections(ACE), which helped to broaden and deepen mass political participatory space, apart from constant and sustained engagement with issues of political education and awareness-raising.

5. The Niger Delta narrative is defined by a problematic trans-ethnic relationship in the Nigerian domestic context, which in turn is underpinned by the representational image of the Self and the Other in a constant search for social, political, cultural and economic justification and legitimation. The conflict spawned by the inter-mix of oil, poverty, underdevelopment, ecological and environmental denudation and mass disempowerment became increasingly radicalized by arms-bearing militants and other discontented locals who began to engage in a wide-range of criminal activities to drive home their point.

6. Ife Agwu, 2000. *Amidst the Blowing Tempest.* Dugbe, Ibadan: John Archers Ltd.

7. The Nigerian Benue Valley States (Benue, Plateau, Nasarawa and Taraba) have been periodically engulfed by intermittent communal and sectarian violent conflicts between 2001 and 2014 that have led to internal displacement, loss of lives, economic and social dislocation and political tension and instability. This phenomenon has also engulfed Borno and Yobe States in Nigeria's North-East region, even assuming a more haunting and tragic spectre of bomb explosions and other newer forms of security threats and challenges spawned by the Boko Haram terrorist organization.

8. Jude C. Ogu. 2007. The Trial of Wazobia. Enugu: ABIC Books Ltd.

9. Wazobia is a coinage from the verb "come" derived from

Nigeria's three man indigenous languages: "Wa" meaning "come" in Yoruba; "Zo" meaning "come" in Hausa and "Bia" meaning "come" in Igbo. Wazobia is representative of Nigerian cultural reality and national identity, and sometimes of the nation's constant and unending search of an elusive theme.
10. Seyi Adigun. 2009. *Prayer for the Mwalimu:* Ibadan: Kraft Books Limited.
11. Mabel Evwierhoma. 2005. *A Song As I am.* Publishing Consultants: Emerald International Development Services (EIDS)
12. Humphrey Onyima. 2009. *21- Gunshots.* Abuja: Ka-yod Graphics
13. Denja Abdullahi. 2008. *Abuja Nunyi.* Ibadan: Kraft Books Limited.
14. Enobong Uwemedimo. *Reminiscences.*
15. J.P Clark. Bedekeremo. *Mandela and Other Poems.* 2003 (rpt). Ikeja, Lagos: Longman Nig. PLC.
16. Niyi Osundare 1999. *The Word is an Egg.* Ibadan: Kraft Books Ltd.
17. J.P Clark-Bekederemo is a foremost First Generation Nigerian dramatist, poet and literary critic. His works include *Poems* (Mbari publications), *A Reed in the Tide* (Longman), *Casualties* (Longman), *A Decade of Tongues* (Longman), *State of the Union* (Longman), *Three Plays* (Oxford), *Ozidi* (Oxford), *The Bikoroa Plays* (Oxford) and *The Wives' Revolt* (University Press Ltd). His critical works include *The Example of Shakespeare* (Longman), and *The Hero as a Villain* (University of Lagos Press). His autobiography is titled *America, Their America* (Andre Deutsch).
18. Niyi Osundare is one of Africa's foremost poets, a dramatist, critic, essayist and media columnist. Many literary scholars believe, and with good reason, that he is a worthy successor to the late Chris Okigbo as Africa's best poet. His published works include: *Songs of the Marketplace* (Ibadan: New Horn Press, 1983); *Village*

Voices (Ibadan: Heinemann, 1986); *Moon Songs* (Ibadan: Spectrum Books, 1988); *Songs of the Season* (Ibadan: Heinemann, 1990); *Waiting Laughters* (Lagos and Oxford: Malthouse press, 1990); *Horses of Memory* (Ibadan: Heinemann,1991); and *Selected Poems* (Oxford: Heinemann International, 1992)

19. K.K. Iloduba. 2007. *In the Arms of Misery*. Apapa, Lagos: Hybun Publications Int. Angela Amosu. 2000. *Waking Dreams*. Apapa, Lagos: Hybun Publications Int.
20. Ken Saro-Wiwa. *Forest of Flowers*.
21. See 19 above.
22. Traditional Swahili poem.
23. Niyi Osundare, Interview with *Sahara Reporters*, 11 January, 2011.
24. Amanze Akpuda, "A Dream Beyond Pyramids: Ferment, Harvest, Bazaar, And Carnival in Nigerian Literature of The Post-Soyinka Nobel Prize Era", *Daily Independent*, 19 August, 2009 p. 9.
25. *Ibid*, p. 8.
26. *Ibid*, pp. 2-4
27. Oyeniyi Okunoye, "Writing Resistance: Dissence and Visions of Healing in Nigerian Poetry of the Military Era", Tydskrif Vir Letter-Kunde. 48(1). 2011, P.65.
28. Ibid, p. 65.
29. Ibid, p. 79.
30. Ibid, p. 80.
31. Some of Niyi Osundare's post-2000 works include: *The Word is an Egg* (Ibadan: Kraft Books, 2000); *Pages from the Book of the Sun: New and Selected Poems* (Trenton, NJ: African World Press, 2002; *Thread in the Loom*: Essays on African Literature and Culture (Trenton, NJ: African World Press, 2002); and *The State Visit* (a play)(Ibadan: Kraft Books, 2002).
32. Tanure Ojaide published the following collections of poems between 1999 and 2008: *When It No Longer Matters Where You Live* (Calabar: University of Calabar: University of Calabar Press, 1999); *Invoking the Warrior*

Spirit: New and Selected Poems (Trenton, NJ: Africa World Press, 1999); *In the Kingdom of Songs*: poems 1995-2000 (Trenton, NJ: Africa World Press, 2002); *I Want to Dance and Other Poems* (San Francisco: African Heritage Press, 2003; *In the House of Words* (Lagos: Malthouse Press Limited 2006); *The Tale of the Harmattan* (Cape Town, S.A: Kwela Books/Snail Press, 2007); and *Waiting For the Hatching of a Cockerel*: a *New Epic Song* (Trenton, NJ: Africa World Press, 2008).

33. Emmanuel Folorunso Taiwo, "A Reading of Yoruba Proverbial as Socio-Political Satire in Osundare's *Waiting Laughters,*" *Lumina*, Vol.12, No. 2, Oct 2010.

34. Uzoechi Nwagbara, "The Antimony of Exile: Ambivalence and Transnational Discontents in Tanure Ojaide's *When It No Longer Matters Where You Live*", *The African Symposium: An Online Journal of the African Educational Research Network.*

35. Aderemi Raji-Oyelade, "Notes Towards the Bibliography of Nigerian Women Poetry (1985-2006); *Research in African Literatures*, Vol.39, No.1, Spring 2008, Pp.183-203. Indeed, a different version of this article also appears as "Representational Exposures: The Album of Nigerian Women Poetry (1985-2006) in C. Maatzke, A. Raji-Oyelade and G.V. Davis eds, *Minstrels and Masks: The Legacy of Ezenwa-Ohaeto in Nigerian Writing*. 2006. New York: Rodopi, pp. 293-316. Of interest too are his "The Virtuous Imagination of a Female Voice in Recent Nigerian Poetry: A reading of Mujidah Aleem's *Another Story*" in *Sermicerchio: Journal of Comparative Literature*, 35.2 (2006), pp.109-110 and *The Post Colonial Lamp*: Essays in Honour of D.S. Izevbaye (2008: Ibadan, Book Kraft) which he edited with Oyeniyi Okunoye. Indeed, the abstract of "Notes Towards the Bibliography of Nigerian Women Poetry (1985-2006)" is worth reproducing here to underscore the author's objective research intentions. "Since the publication of Ifi Amadiume's Passion Waves (1985), so many

remarkable, single-authored volumes have appeared on the Nigerian Literary scene that it has become necessary to attempt a bibliographic count of the many collections produced by women authors in the past two decades. In a general sense, so much discourse of contemporary African literature has underrepresented the works of the few women poets on the continent that the appearance of the Heinemann's *Book of African Women's Poetry* by Stella and Frank Chipasula in 1995 was a salutary textual turn towards a revisionist scholarship of postcolonial African poetry.

36. Ismail Bala, "Women Poetry from Northern Nigeria: A Bibliographic Note", *Gender and Behaviour*, Dec, 2010 (http:/www.faas.org/periodicals/201012/2187713.321.html).

Apart from the article's very useful references and pointers for further reading, it also brings together 38 collections of poems written by female writers published between 1996 and 2008. In the words of the author: "...this is a pioneering effort to record all published books of poems by women from Northern Nigeria... The bibliographic note is principally concerned with books by women, since it is more likely to have more male poets than female, and also because female poets, at least those using the English Language in Northern Nigeria have a late start; the earliest book by a female poet here is only published in 1996". And concerning, the gap she wants to fill, the author declares as follows: "many critics have described what is often called 'the zero presence' of the female voice in Nigerian poetry: Nigerian female writers trail behind their male counterparts for a number of reasons (literary, historical and cultural). This is more pronounced if not more acute in Northern Nigeria, where literature of English expression is slow in evolving, compared to other parts of the country. Poetry of English expression by women from Northern Nigeria is indeed young, and is written in a tradition that is not only new but developing".

37. See for example, Oyeniyi Okunoye's "Alterity, Marginality and the National Question in the Poetry of the Niger Delta", *Cahiers D'Etudes Africaines*, 13 (No. 19, 2008). The author declares that his main research quest is informed by the following: "In a bid to confirm the growing complexity of African literary geography and also extend the scholarly engagement of the experience of the Niger Delta Region of Nigeria to the cultural sphere, the paper draws attention to the unique poetic tradition that the region sustains. Underscoring the enduring concern with the link between humanity and nature in the creative imagination of poets from the Niger Delta. It establishes continuity between the efforts of older poets like Gabriel Okara and J.P. Clark, and those of Ken Saro-Wiwa, Tanure Ojaide, Martins Adiyi-Bestman, and Ibiwari Ikiriko. Utilizing insights drawn from minority discursive practices and the strategy of close reading in constructing a trans-ethnic literary tradition", the paper examines the "articulate expressions of the poetry of the Niger Delta, privileging the collective drama and contestations of the people...: insistence on registering the otherness of the Niger Delta within Nigeria and the consequent interrogation of the Nigerian project..." See also Eldred Ibibiem Grien and Seiyifa Koroye, "Literature of the Izon". This is a useful research resource, detailing as it does, an extensive examination of all facets of Ijaw literary craft, especially poetry, past and present.

38. Sule E. Egya, "Art and Outrage: A Critical Survey of Recent Nigerian Poetry in English", *Research in African Literatures*, Vol. 42, No. 1 (Spring 2011, pp. 49-67). In the words of the author: "This essay is an attempt to map out their (the poets of the late 1980s and 1990s, and the necessary precursor of the poetic vision and craft of the post-2000 poets) artistic endeavours, the

tradition from which they emerge, the social context of their poetry and their collective contribution to the discourse of nationhood in Nigeria during the struggles to unseat military despotism. The essay contends that although this "new poetry" is not fundamentally different form the poetry that emerged in the post-independence era in Nigeria, it has its peculiar features as an artistic response to a particular period of anomie".
39. S.S. Olaoluwa, "African Poetry and the Politics of Exile: A Critical Survey"...
40. Chin Ce, "Four Decades of African Poetry," Journal of African Poetry (from Essays in Literature, African Book Networks<http://www.hbooknetworks.com/Cnz.htm)
41. GMT Emezue, "History, Vision and craft in New Nigerian Poetry", p.1, 2005.
42. Ibid, pp. 1-2
43. Ibid, p. 2.
44. Senator Ihenyem, "Contemporary Nigerian Poetry– Which Way Forward?" *African Writer Co.*

Part Six

POETRY AND POLITICS IN APARTHEID SOUTH AFRICA

Modern South African poetry, just as its prose and dramatic counterparts, is a direct response to existential impulses conditioned by the deliberate barbarization of the individual in what was the then apartheid system. Essentially a literature of exile at its emergence, imaginative works by South Africans strive to recall the structure of alienated living in an environment previously used to racial inequality and political oppression. Poetry is one medium of rallying people at home to mobilize for the inevitable confrontation with racism, and a message to the outside world about injustice at home. Increasingly, though, the second position indicated in the premise indicated above seems to dominate as class consciousness grows, as underground publishing houses sprout up and as the tempo of political agitation increases. South African poets, even with the dismantling of apartheid, are speaking to their people now as much as they are speaking to outsiders.

From the nascent days of the formation of structures of apartheid and its wide-ranging institutions of organized dehumanization of individuals to the present time of fundamental changes engendered by the world democratic process,[1] changes which have dismantled the foundation of racial apartness, South African poets have consistently shown a remarkable grasp of the social processes at work in their society, understand the individual responses to the pressures of existence and underscore the potential inherent in building a revolutionary tradition of struggle.

Apartheid as a social system and as part of the world system of international imperialism lent itself to the stereotyping and simplification of phenomena, and created the conditions necessary for the generation, development and perpetuation of myths, dogmas and illusions. It is a mark of the vital creative strength and energy of South African poets, and an indication of their humanism and acute creative imagination, that in their presentations of the glaring horrors of apartheid, they still apprehend and mediate the subtle shades of consciousness, feelings and emotions of the oppressors and do not allow their art to degenerate to the level of being a naturalistic, photographic and illustrationist one-on-one correspondence with material reality. One can even assert that there is a more healthy mix of art and ideology in South African poetry, with all the complexes, agonies and traumas of that society, than in any other part of Africa where situations are marginally better.

From the poetry of Vilakazi[2] to the present-day effort of Wally Serote and Sipho Sepamla, the ideo-aesthetic of South African poetry has in the main been undergirded by the persistent socio-political reality of the erstwhile apartheid system. Responses to this all-pervading phenomenon varied from poet to poet, from collection to collection, and from poem to poem, depending on the private and social circumstances of the composition and the creative process which is part of the artistic individuality of the poet. We cannot neatly classify South African poets into the category of those whose works purvey a liberal outlook, and who work under a critical realist context and those whose works purvey radical tendencies and who subscribe to the tenets of revolutionary aesthetics. The reason for this classificatory difficulty is the complex nature of the South African poet who combines the qualities of radical liberalism and revolutionary enthusiasm in different poems and collections, and at different stages of his artistic development.

South African poetry has attracted much deserved attention, and despite the subjectivist, sometimes self-opinionated and mischief-making research efforts of scholars, the overall picture is that of a vibrant poetic tradition that has flowered to full maturity and which is captured in all its diversity, multiplicity and many sidedness. It is important, in this regard, to make mention of some of the major studies on South African poetry as a way of a proper contextualization of that ideo-aesthetic tradition, and a way of pointing out to future researchers some of the relevant literature in the field. We have, as ready points of reference, O.R. Dathorne's conservative survey-summary method in "African Poetry in English" in his *African Literature in the 20th Century*[3] where he devotes space to the study of Dennis Brutus, Keroapetse Kgositsile and Mazisi Kunene. Adrian Roscoe's "Aspects of South African Verse" in his *Uhuru's Fire: African Literature East to South*[4] also treats Vilakazi and Brutus in the pattern adopted by Dathorne. We also have the very original but controversial article by Bahadur Tejani, "Can a Prisoner Make a Poet?: Note on a Reading of Dennis Brutus' "Letters to Martha" in *African Literature Today*, No.6[5] which has generated one of the most sustained and interesting arguments in the development of African literature on the vital issues of art and ideology; the role of the artist in the mobilization of the people; and the place of private thoughts and emotions in the revolutionary process. One of the more interesting responses to Bahadur's article is Romanus Egudu's "Pictures of Pain: The Poetry of Dennis Brutus," in *Perspectives on South African Literature*,[6] an interesting collection that contains other relevant articles on the issues of poetry and politics in South Africa. Some other responses to Tejani's article include J.M. Salt, "On the Business of Literary Criticism: Comments on B. Tejani's "Can a Prisoner Make a Poet," in *African Literature Today* No.6[7] and V.U. Ola's "The Neglected Dimension in the Poetry of Dennis Brutus", in *Njala*.[8] V.U. Ola also has an article on O.M. Mtshali, "The Poet and his Message: The Poetry of O.M. Mtshali" which appeared in a 1984 issue of *AMAN*.[9]

The literary arguments and discussions in these articles and many others which are not mentioned contribute significantly to the sustenance of the examination of the South African poetic tradition and the continued evolution of radical and committed scrutiny of its ideo-aesthetic ontology. Recently, Ezenwa-Ohaeto has come out with a very illuminating comparative piece on Taban L.O. Liyong and Sipho Sepamla, while Wally Serote in a 1988 round table discussion with Ngugi wa Thiong'o and a panel of African National Congress activists[10] sheds more light on not only his poetry but also on the whole range of revolutionary literature in South Africa.

As has already been mentioned, most of these critical beam lights on South African poetry is a sign that there is a thriving poetic consciousness among the South Africans as most of the comments are very favourable, and not in any patronizing or paternalistic dimension. It is not possible to list all the major works in the area; neither is it possible to study any of them in-depth. What we have done is to map the broad contours of this aesthetic site by briefly looking at one or two poems of Dennis Brutus and Oswald Mbuyiseni Mtshali who are representative of South African poets and use that to project a generalized ideo-aesthetic comment on the entire corpus of South African poetry.

Writing about the essential qualities of Dennis Brutus' poetry and the source of his strength as a poet, Adrian Roscoe says:

> "So much of the poetry of Dennis Brutus... is marked by modesty and reason. It is remarkable that a man who has suffered the worst inhumanities which white men have inflicted on Africa, including forced labour and a bullet in the back, should protest in so quiet a

voice, in such measured tones, in such unpretentious verse. Where violence or screaming despair might be appropriate for an artist in Brutus' position, his characteristic response blends dignity with patience, and calmness with reason, determined always that emotionalism must never triumph. Even when his oppressors are discomfited, we find modest joy rather than thumping triumphalism, joy that is almost embarrassed and self-conscious".[11]

O.R. Dathorne's observations that Brutus "does not preach, his work has a rare economy of diction that says just so much and no more,"[12] is very similar to Roscoe's assertion. It is this tendency to control his emotions, to obscure and mask his feelings, to retain and express his humanity subtly, and to understand the dilemma of even the oppressors that J.M. Salt, R.N. Egudu and V.U. Ola all stress in the articles already mentioned. It is some of these qualities, including his apparent incapacity to declare an open political stance; the personalized nature of the apprehended and mediated experience; his hesitations and seeming indecision in the face of an obscurantist oppressive ideology; the apologetic tone of some of the poems; and the somewhat liberal humanist ideals as against revolutionary sentiments expressed in them that attracted Tejani's censure. One can, of course, argue that Roscoe, Dathorne, Salt, Egudu and Ola are sympathetic to Brutus and analyze his work favourably principally because they subscribe to the spirit of liberalism his poetry is infused with, and endorse the gradualist approach to the solution of South African sociopolitical, economic and ideological crisis which his poetry seems to emphasize.

A good point in looking at the poetry of Dennis Brutus[13] could be this statement by V.U. Ola:

> Most of the poetry of Brutus is typified by (the) mixture of pain and joy in living which creates the impression that the poet is less interested in

rendering the screams and yells of suffering humanity than in the belief that the human spirit has an unfathomable capability to wheather such pains, hence his consistent forward-looking posture in the poems.[14]

The assertion, without doubt, is a penetrating analysis of the dominant features of Brutus' poetry. In his grappling with the South African situation, Brutus reaches deep down into the deepest recess of the human soul to discover love, compassion and understanding amid the surface staccato noise of despair and pain, and the insensate bestiality of his world.

In "A Troubadour I Traverse...", he pictures himself as a roving bard, touring the whole expanse of South Africa, protesting about her humiliation and singing songs of courage and hope to his oppressed countrymen and women. By using medieval allusion of an European poet-knight protecting his lady from the Moslem Saracens, Brutus is thus showing us the compatibility of loving and fighting, singing and struggling:

> A troubadour, I traverse all my land...
> and have laughed, disdaining those
> who banned inquiry and movement, delighting
> in the test of will when doomed by
> saracened arrest...

At this point, there is a marked spirit of defiance and courage when, despite the arrest and torture, he still chooses, "like unarmed thumb, simply to stand". Brutus is stressing the basic fact of existence that love cannot be sacrificed for an abstract humanity, that compassion can only be meaningful when it is predicated on the solid ground of mutual understanding. In essence, the very barbarity of the South African apartheid system will engender nothing but discord, anarchy and instability and can only attract stout resistance and determined opposition by all morally conscious people, no matter their degree of tolerance and their capacity for patience and endurance.

Through the image of the laughable Don Quixote, the hero of the 16th century prose narrative of that name by Cervantes, Brutus points at the difficulty involved in accomplishing his task. However, the optimism in the poem is face saving, forced and unrealistic to an extent because "no mistress favour (for a good work done) has adorned my breast/only the shadow of an arrow brand" (gunshot wounds and other scars of racist torture). Brutus has effectively brought out his poetic vision of political savagery in South Africa, even when working through a complex pattern of historicized allusion, using both the technical and rhyming sonnet form, and symbolic imagery (of lover and singer) that apparently have nothing in common with the reality of his traumatized land.

In "After Exile" (4 selections), he presents a composite picture of life as a black man in South Africa. Section one in particular is imagistic – specific and historic, natural and universal. The first stanza shows the metaphoric relationship between the obstinate resistance of a tree to the elemental forces and the stubborn courage displayed by the harassed blacks:

> I am the tree
> Creaking in the wind
> Outside in the night
> twisted and stubborn.

The metaphoric pattern continues where the poet compares himself to a twisted sheet that nevertheless "grates" in the wind/in a shrill sad protest," while the "voice" is very universal, symbolizing the utterance of everybody who feels disquieted at the inhumanity of man to man in South Africa:

> I am the voice
> Crying in the night
> that cries endlessly
> and will not be consoled.

The whole complex range of Dennis Brutus' poetry, contained in over four volumes and scattered in hundreds of journals, cannot be summarized in just a page or so as I have attempted to do. What we have done is to give a few broad strokes about the direction of his creative quest, underscore some of the basic ideo-aesthetic features of his art and point out some of the critical beam lights on him. This will serve as a basis for a further and fuller exploration of his aesthetic method and social concern, and as a basis for inter-textual analysis[15].

Oswald Mbuyiseni Mtshali, one of the younger South African poets; that is, if we consider the generation of Brutus, Lewis Nkosi, Eskia Mphalele and Mazisi Kunene, apprehends the necessity of protest against apartheid through irony, contrast, gentle sarcastic humour, gripping imagery and a heavy reliance on personification. In "Nightfall in Soweto", he presents a picture of blacks crudely crushed by the apartheid agents at the fall of night. 'Nightfall' in this poem assumes a symbolic and personified quality because of its representation of political criminality and evil. Moreover, through the use of haunting image wasting disease:

> Nightfall comes like a dreaded disease seeping through the pores of a healthy body and raving it beyond repair...

Of predatory animals and their preys:

> Man has ceased to be man
> Man has become beast
> Man has become prey

And the personification of nightfall as a maleficent agent through rhetorical questions:

> Nightfall! Nightfall!!
> You are my mortal enemy
> But why were u ever created?
> Why can't it be day time
> Daytime for ever more?

Mtshali shocks us into a realization of the trepidation, fear, hopelessness ("in my helplessness I languish") and certain death ("thirsty for my blood") that are the lot of the majority black population in the country of their birth.

In "Just a Passerby", a highly ironic and sarcastic poem, Mtshali condemns the escapist and mute indifferent attitude to political murder as a consequence of the uncritical acceptance of the doctrines and dogmas of Christianity. Christianity in this poem is seen as a demeaning and reactionary doctrine that destroys the individual's capacity for resistance or active participation in the fight for liberation:

> I saw them clobber him with Kieries,
> I heard him scream with pain
> Like a victim of slaughter
> I smelt fresh blood gush
> From his nostrils
> And flow on the street

This is a charged emotive presentation of horror, using graphic imagistic patterns and play on words 'slaughter' is a word meant for beasts and not man', that evokes in us the feeling of repulsion at the bestial injustice of the action:

> I walked into the church
> and knelt in the pew
> "Lord! I love you
> I also love my neighbour, Amen"

This is a sharp and marked contrast to the first stanza because of the deliberate way and manner the narrator's emotion is presented. Love is perverted, abstracted and meaningless if it cannot compel one to protect his kinsman. When the narrator is re-told this horrifying deed by his "woman neighbour" he cries: "O! No! I heard nothing/ I have been to church". Mtshali thus utilizes basic poetic devices – captivating imagery, gripping irony and sarcasm, play on words and personification – to drive home his picture of political reality in South Africa, a reality that is as terrifying as it is revolting.

Most of O.M. Mtshali's poems are collected in *Sounds of A Cowhide Drum*,[16] from where the above two poems are selected. Oswald Mtshali is a very vibrant poet whose idiom and social vision is closer to the revolutionary aesthetic of the younger South African poets (Sipho Sepamla and Wally Serote) than to the liberal imagination of Brutus and Arthur Nortje. Mtshali has been accused of indecisiveness and irresolution in the face of the challenge mounted by apartheid. Some of his poems are really escapist in nature, displaying an indifference to and lack of concern for positive action against apartheid, but others really work because in the poet's concern with the agonies of living under the system, he makes poignant statements above life and experience.

This brief treatment of South African poetry is part of a continuing research effort to properly understand the nature of the South African experience and the role played by protest poetry in apprehending that reality and arousing the consciousness of the oppressed to fight against their oppressors. His socio-political situation in South Africa is very dynamic and revolutionary and with the sustained pressure of internal protest and dissent and external diplomatic, political and considerable economic pressures, the structures and institutions of apartheid had come trembling down, to be replaced by black majority rule under Nelson Mandela. It is of course, surprising to many skeptics that we are already talking and writing about post-protest and post-apartheid poetry in South Africa, and talking and writing about poetry directed towards the reconstruction of the society along the path of peace, progress and true democracy. But this is the reality as we know it today, and a reality already complicated by the debate over postcoloniality and post-modern consciousness in the new, post-apartheid South African poetry; an ontological and aesthetic phenomenon which the next part of this study will investigate in some detail.

Notes and References

1. Nelson Mandela has already been freed, the ban of the ANC lifted, and a national unity government was elected in April 1994 under his leadership.
2. Vilakazi was one of the earliest modern South African poets, and though his poetry has obvious socio-aesthetic limitations, he influenced an entire generation of South African poets.
3. "African Poetry in English" in *African Literature in the 20th Century*.
4. (London: Cambridge Univ. Press, 1976).
5. "(London: Heinemann, 1975).
6. *Aspects of South Africa Literature*, (London: Heinemann, 1976).
7. *African Literature Today*, No. 6 (1975).
8. "The Neglected Dimension in the Poetry of Dennis Brutus", *NJALA*, No. 4, Vol. 3, 1984.
9. "The Poet and His Message: The Poetry of Oswald M. Mtshali", *AMAN*, 1984.
10. "Black Consciousness in East/South African Poetry," *Presence Africaine*, No. 140 (4th quarterly), 1986.
11. *The Africa Communist*, Vol. 3 No. 4 (1985).
12. *Uhuru's Fire*, pp. 157-158
13. *African Literature in the 20th Century*, p. 214.
14. Some of the collected poetry of Dennis Brutus are *Siren, Knuckles and Boots, A Simple Lust* and *Letters to Martha*.
15. "The Neglected Dimension in the poetry of Dennis Brutus" p. 46.
16. *Sounds of a Cowhide Drum* (Johannesburg: Restnor Publishers, 1971).

Part Seven

SOUTH AFRICAN POETRY AFTER 1994 AND THE POSTCOLONIAL DEBATE

Introduction

There are a lot of linkages and connections, at various levels and in different contexts, between parts six and seven of this discourse. This much is also noted with regard to parts four and five. My initial research strategy was to unite part seven with part six in a continuous and seamless analytic flow, but on second thought I pursued an investigation of the post-apartheid, postcolonial South African poetry to a considerable depth as part of the project of bringing out the work's second edition. The implication is that while historical, aesthetic and ideological overlaps exist between the two, the intent is to further clarify, systematize and elaborate on my earlier research quest in the new discourse.

Written postcolonial South African poetry in English refers to poetry written by South African citizens after 1994, the liberation year when the flag of apartheid was lowered and that of multi-racial democracy hoisted. The poetic creations of this period represents sufficient and interesting corpus of literary output, deserving of penetrating scholarly attention in its own right such that it is tempting to proceed to delve into it without reference to the poetry ante-dating it, and which shows the rough road trod to get to the contemporary state of things. As may well be known, South Africa occupies a prime place in modern African poetry's origin, being the home of the first two African poets of English expression, Nsikana, whose hymnal verses written in the 1920s earned him commendation as "the first African bard"[1] as well as H.E.B. Dhlomo, whose book-length poem *"The Valley of a Thousand Hills"* (1945) earned accolades from the colonial critics as the "first African to compose a modern poem in the white man's tongue"[2]. These pioneer attempts at poetic creation by Nsikana and Dhlomo, with clear functional and artistic merits, marked the foundation of modern African poetry of English expression and bridged the gap between Africa traditional oral poetic aesthetics and African contemporary poetry written in the borrowed language of English in terms of expressive styles and idiom. The significance of these early attempts by Africans which were inserted into the dominant colonial ideological and aesthetic moment did more than deconstruct contemporary colonial disparaging myth about Africans, as a people with no creative imagination.[3]

Izibolongo Tradition of Poetry

The earliest manifestation of written South African poetry on a corpus scale is represented by the *Izibolongo* tradition, so called because, functionally and artistically, the new poetry was influenced by *izibolongo,* the indigenous poetic art of Izimbongi, the popular South African native poetic craft of the Zulu and Xhosa people who composed *imbingi* poetry in praise of their leaders. The contemporary *izibolongo* poetry was written by the first group of South Africans exposed to Western education and culture, including E.E.N. Nkize, A. M. Nzimande and Nichodemus Zungu. This poetry was written in the English language which the poets learnt in the colonial mission schools. In addition, it appropriated traditional Zulu and Xhosa poetry, technically and functionally, making full use of indigenous aesthetic and communication resources, such as tones, call and response, chorus, repetition, echo, intonation, and song.[4]

However, the expanse of their social function remains the confident affirmation and validation of authentic African institutions and traditions, the celebration of the biodiversity and rich cultural and ecological landscape of South Africa, and the preservation of African traditional and cultural heritage, before the tidal wave of colonialism wiped everything away. Herein lies its significant contribution to South African poetic and literary culture. Its originality and heritage value can also be inferred from its shadowy influence on the incantatory style of South African poets of the oral school such as Mazizi Kunene and Oswald Mtshali.

Apartheid Phase

Apartheid, a political system in South Africa from 1948 to 1994, and which separated South Africans along colour lines, gave privileges to people of European origin, and denied people of African descent political, social and economic rights. It generated the corpus of South Africa poetry written between 1950 and 1993, generally christened anti-apartheid poetry. As the name implies, anti-apartheid poetry was written as part of the cultural and aesthetic ideology of the then contemporary political and physical struggle against apartheid, which was led by the African National Congress (ANC), a revolutionary political organization founded in 1912 that worked to promote the interests of black Africans.

As the apartheid authorities worked to secure a stranglehold on South Africa through repressive legislations that scuttled conventional politically organized opposition against it, the intellectual elite resorted to using poetry and other modes of artistic expressions, as an effective and suitable tool for commentary and criticism,[5] to fight the government. Naturally the authorities responded with impunity by banning their works, blanket-wise, within South Africa, hounding poets into exile, and clamping many more in jail. Others who could not endure the harsh conditions at home immigrated to countries outside South Africa that shared the concrete objectives and goals of the liberation struggle and continued to write from there.

Anti-apartheid poetry fought apartheid by exposing the injustices in the system both to South Africans and the outside world, thereby engaging and enlisting the attention, sympathy and support of the international community in the efforts to eradicate it. In doing so, the poetry came to be a prototype of the poetry of liberation that had been written in countries like Chile, Mozambique, Portuguese Guinea and Guyana by Pablo Neruda, Agostinho Neto, Amilcar Cabral and Martin Carter, when their own countries were under the inauspicious political, economic and cultural circumstances that South Africans found themselves.

Notable anti-apartheid poets like Peter Martins, Sardie Nkondo, Breyten Breytenbach, Dennis Brutus, Oswald Mtshali, Mazisi Kunene and Arthur Nortje are as daring as they are imaginative. The themes they explored in their works are strongly rooted in the sufferings caused by apartheid, while their language is robustly critical of apartheid. In all their works, they used deep tones, picturesque images and suggestive language to illuminate the unsavoury reality around them. The political consciousness in the poetry of the period, in terms of the poetic function and vision to raise public awareness about the troubled times, and sensitize the people about their social predicament and realities, is evident in Walter Nhlapo's "The Revolution Song", which sends poetry forth to the world as a messenger of freedom:

> Go across the desert and the sea,
> And sing, "Black men shall be free!
> Go everywhere beneath the sun
> Join all black soul into one
> (Nhlapo's "The Revolution Song", excerpt)

The central message of the poem is the rallying call of all black people both within and outside South Africa to raise the trenchant banner of the anti-apartheid struggle. The declaration – "All black men shall be free" – pre-empts the tone of urgency, militancy and defiance which typifies anti-apartheid poetry. Despite the deadly political terrain, the rest of the poets had to follow the example of Walter Nhlapo in churning out poetry sometimes considered political songs, but which is clearly not lacking in inspiration and aesthetic direction as a component of the cultural and ideological struggle to change the socio-political and economic structure of South Africa. The suffering and hopelessness of the times, and the resultant mood of bleakness, despair and misery evident all over South Africa, found expression in waves of restiveness, anxiety and sporadic pseudo-racial attacks triggered by the polarization of society along racial lines, and often times, marked by intense inter-racial rivalry, bitterness and conflicts.

The cruelty and ruthlessness of the apartheid leaders propelled by the unflinching zeal to maintain the status quo, pervades the themes of Dennis Brutus' poetry. In his *Letters to Martha* (1970), the poet develops two dimensions of this cruelty and ruthlessness; namely, prison, confinement and torture. Historically speaking, during apartheid, a person can be arrested and jailed anytime as a prisoner of conscience. He or she may be locked away indefinitely for years behind bars without the ritual of fair trial, with torture, physically, mentally and psychologically, inflicted on him, in order to compel a stoppage of his anti-apartheid activities, as the case of Nelson Mandela who was jailed for 27 years in Robben Island maximum security prison in order to break his resistance spirit, indicates. In "On the Islands", the isolation of prison life fuses with the elements of weather, while Robben Island itself becomes a metaphor of misery for prisoners of conscience in apartheid jails. In "Letter 9", for instance, Brutus talks about the inhuman treatment received by apartheid's prisoners, capturing their sufferings and the lingering tough times that further mar their ding-dong life:

> Cement grey time
> And grey susurration
> Of the seas breaking
> Winds blowing
> And rains drizzling
> Cement grey floors
> Cement grey ....

Brutus' poetry never lacks a deep concern for human waste, the greatest foible of apartheid, and the misery of oppression and prison. He uses concrete images and symbols suggesting death to secure an identity for apartheid Africa as an epitome of waste and void. The searing pain and misery captured in Brutus' poems inspired their description as poetic "art hammered out of pain"[6]. The same caustic depiction of pain and misery also inspired Trevor's remark that the poetry of Brutus aptly demonstrates:

> Acute sensitivity shaped by the apartheid experience; responsiveness to human drama and beauty; anger that resonates with a sense of prophetic fury as well as ability to extract pattern from pain and experience[7]

The maltreatment and repression of blacks, largely institutionalized as state policy through unjust back-up legislations were, on the whole, realized to be counter-productive as it paradoxically and inadvertently sparked concomitant violent response from the side of blacks who were desperate to effect change, in the form of defiance, civil disobedience and revolutionary insurgency. Paradigms of this are thematized in Arthur Nortje's poetry. In "Boy on a Swing", the prevalent spate of extrajudicial killings and indiscriminate jailing that darkened life under apartheid is deftly hinted at, and challenged via the involuntary vision and non-liable, commandeering acts of a child dizzy with play but fully aware and educated enough to question:

> Slowly he moves
> to and fro, to and fro

> then faster and faster
> he swishes up and down
>
> His blue shirt
> billows in the breeze
> like a tattered kite
>
> The world whirls by;
> east becomes west,
> north turns to south
> the four cardinal points
> meet in his head
>
> Mother!
> Where did I come from?
> When will I wear long trousers?
> Why was my father jailed?
> (Arthur Nortje "Boy on a Swing", full text)

The strident fretting and complaining widespread in South Africa during apartheid era is latent in the poem, along with hard criticism and subtle prophesy conveying the imminent doom of apartheid. Its visual language is hushed in terms that suggest that though their voices have been taken away, the blacks never relinquished their capacity or willpower to question the system. Anxiety may be underscored by interrogations coming from the innocent boy, but a note of defiance is latent in the heroic and intellectual cross-examination of the system, insipidly evil and entrenched. And, because it lacks any moral credential and basis of defense and/or continuity, it literarily crumbles under the weight of its own misdeeds.

The poetry of South Africa at this point in time fits squarely in the general conception of poetry as a veritable instrument of political and social struggle. Then, South Africa, according to S. Raditholo, was a house that was burning, and it was possibly the prime task of the writer to "help douse the flame in order to ensure the social and cultural survival of her people"[8]. Suffice it to say that in the South African political and social context of apartheid, nothing much of poetry would be considered "which was not the eyes and ears of the revolution"⁹. The need to be on the side of the people against the forces that oppress them clearly underlines the positive role the poets played as active and meaningful change agents during apartheid.

Post-Apartheid Phase

Since liberation in 1994, the pattern of poetry has changed, aided by the meeting of minds on the synchronic discourse on the question of art and national reconstruction in postcolonial South Africa. The general consensus is that to speedily reconstruct the ruins apartheid caused, South Africa needs all hands on deck. Coincidentally, in the post-liberation era, the art of poetry and the personality of the poet have become infused with huge ethical and ideological weight. Among the literati and audiences alike, poetry is complimentarily regarded as amenable to a more sublime and insightful "truth" than political discourse, or even social commentary, an incisive discourse, potentially free of cant with deceit, and the poet seen as a unique outlet of authenticity, vision and "truth" — including social truths — invisible to others.[10]

Baleka Mbete openly popularizes the pride of associating with poetry, declaring that the best compliment he may wish to receive is to be addressed as a poet. Even non-poets, like Hermann Mashaba, a Cape Town businessman, argues that the entrepreneur is "the poet of the private sector", and adds, "if we want the Western Cape to be a home for all, maybe we must ask our poets to pick up where we couldn't. We need to usher in an era of our poets again."[11]

Although the new poetry shifted focus from the racially charged past with its old themes of political struggle, it does not pretend to shy away from the immediate social and economic issues thrust forth by the democratic system, such as equity, justice, and fairness. Thus, even though the poets are not unified by a common functional or artistic ideology but wrote as poets with individualized ethos, they are still politically engaged, as they reflected upon, and tried to influence the ongoing processes in the country's wider sociocultural and political life.

A direct consequence of multi-racial democracy in South Africa is the immediate increase in literary ferment. With apartheid gone and freedom of expression restored, literary space widened considerably and, in the area of poetry, new writers moved in to articulate issues side by side with the established ones, resulting into a deluge of heritage poetry, rich in thematic diversity, and stylistically variegated as well. It is possible and worthwhile to attempt a categorization of the poetry of the period, with an insight into its ideo-aesthetic and thematic orientation. There are poets who continue to focus on politics, not as social critics but as moral primogenitors who want to point the way towards public morality, and show how individuals, corporate groups and pubic officers should behave. Poets like Sankie Mthembi-Mahanyele, Vusi Mavimbela, Matthews Phosa, Lindiwe Mabuza, Seitlhamo Motsapi, Lisa Combrink, Lance Mogorosi Nawa, Ingrid de Kok, Nise Malange, Mzwakhe Mbuli and Dennis Brutus belong to this group. This coterie of poets have, since 1994, written poems encouraging national reconstruction and nation-building. Mongane Serote, for example, has consistently used his poetry to inveigh the role he has had to play while in public office promoting "reconciliation". In his epic poem "Freedom, Lament and Song", he poeticizes the corruption in post-apartheid South Africa:

> At the big house
> at this HQ of God, Cape Town
> I listen, I look, I touch
> there are liars
> cheats and betrayers
> they maneuver
> they are like vacuum cleaners
> like hyenas
> in their speeches

Evidence of corruption mentioned by the poet in the poem include perjury, dishonesty, promise defaulting, and devious acts of manipulation. Although the poet does not say who "they" refers to, it is clear that he is talking about politicians and public functionaries manning key positions in the new multi-racial government of South Africa. The poet's obvious critical comment inputted in the satirical expression "they maneuver/ they are like vacuum cleaners/ like hyenas/ in their speeches" suggests that these privileged South Africans are entirely corrupt; they take advantage of their exalted positions to deceive the masses with promises calculated to fail, and by acting in ways contrary to promises made.

Dennis Brutus, in his last curtain collections, *Still the Sirens* (2003), *Remembering Soweto* (2004), *Leaf Drift* (2005) and *Wind-drift* (2005) uses images of drift and tragic memorabilia to warn of the likelihood of political and social upheavals resurfacing in the new South Africa if the treachery and excesses of politicians continue unchecked, while Jeremy Cronin wrote poems that ignite public debate and critical reflection on key government policies and strategic economic options involving ANC-led government policies and World Bank, International Monetary Fund, and South African Reserve Bank; the South African State's post-1996 Growth Employment and Redistribution economic policy; the socialist pedigree of privatization policies in China; and the role of the new black middle class in the emerging South Africa.

There are, also, poets whose poems are marked by globules of rage and criticism against the post-liberation order for perceived social contradictions. Frustration and disillusionment arising from the perception that freedom and democracy did not bring about equity and fairness in the distribution of political and economic opportunities inspire the themes explored. Poets like Peter Horn, Kgalela Magogodi, Vonam Bila and Lesego Rampolokeng represent these poets who, according to Vennon Bila, write to fight those:

> Frustrating any efforts to achieve the kind of just society that they spoke about and if that's not bad enough, worse is the fact that while they can see people living in poverty, near starvation, sickness without medical care, homelessness — they can live in disgusting affluence without a sense of guilt.[12]

Unlike the poets of the past, these poets chose as their artistic subjects, not the intelligentsia, not the high profile socialite or literary elite, but the ordinary man in the street, preaching and helping to bring people together in unity and hope. The meta-language of their craft and the defining specificities of their artistic vocation is summed up in Peter Horn's "Bargain Prices":

> Poems? You want poem? We got poems!
> Poems to make you dream ...
> Poems which will disturb you
> Poems
> You do not want to hear this poem?
> They will come to you nevertheless
> (Peter Horn's "Bargain Prices", excerpt)

The poem seems friendly, but the threat it issues to those who short-change the masses, while their perverse interests remain sacrosanct, can be deduced from its ominous and sinister tone. It conveys the growing restiveness which will turn the political and social landscape into a sepulcher burning with terrorism, militancy and political fire; something akin to the Niger Delta militancy and Boko Haram insurgency and other violent non-state actors spouting up here and there in Nigeria, ostensibly, in reaction to the nation's unbroken history of kleptomaniac governance, corruption, hypocrisy, insensitivity, moral ambivalence and ethical inertia.

The image of the poet as a social activist, an advocate of social change, and the voice of the oppressed is most glaring in the poetry of Rampolokeng, particularly in the rabid collections *Horns for Hondo, Talking Rain,* and *Bavino*

Sermons. The eerie titles of the three suggest that all is not well for the "rainbow nation" despite the loud songs of freedom. There is a sense in which Rampolokeng's poetry is truly representative of South African poets raised and bred in the upturned Soweto ghettos of South Africa, a sensibility continuously agitated by the vision of the common man unending Sisyphean struggle against neo-colonialism, represented by the new South African power establishment. The influence of this phantom beast can be seen in the untoward conduct of fellow South Africans fortunate to inherit the reins of power from the eased out apartheid politicians, only to abuse it. The poets' redeeming mission is captured in Rampolokeng's autobiographic comment: "I remain my peoples' transmitter/ this is the reason for my presence"[13], which set the tone for the other poets. In "Rap 3i", Rampolokeng announces himself fully:

> I'm the glittering spectacle
> To battle the censor tentacle
> I came like a release
> From the depression disease
>
> I write to fight
> To make a dark land bright
> (*Bavino Sermons*, 55, excerpt)

The poem's message reflects the cynicism that has become widespread in South Africa, even as apartheid had let go, signifying that the land is simply dark (oppressive), and the poet is destined to make it bright (free). The complexity of Rampolokeng's verse, including sharp and unorthodox hypertexts, incongruous structures, truncated rhyme, Blakean imagery, and mystical allusions reflect the dilemma of South Africa as a society in transition riddled with corruption, hypocrisy and insensitivity, and fraught with abundant social contradictions and human predicaments. The misery of the times is discernible from the dysfunctional mode of the poet's idiom: even rhyme, poetry's best element of musical pleasure, is circumscribed for ideological effect.

Other poets like Mbongeni Khumalo have reacted with suspicion to the gradual erosion of the values of freedom in most African countries involved in the dull enterprise of nation-building. Sharp criticism is, on occasion, heaped on the most hallowed institutions of post-apartheid South Africa, including what Lesego Rampolokeng calls South Africa's "malice-in-wonderland" Constitution ("Rap" 30).

In some poems, such as Chris Mann's "Where is the Freedom for Which They Died?" the names of heroes and martyrs of the anti-apartheid struggle are used as a comparative counterpoint to shame other South Africans involved in internecine conflict, family abuse and violence. In others, such as Karen Press' "Tiresias in the City of Heroes" and Bila's "Mandela, Have You Ever Wondered?", archetypal images are used to highlight the degree to which a country awash with nationalist rhetoric has accepted old habits that do not challenge people's preconceptions of, or responses to the structures of power, as Siphiwe ka Ngwenya does in "Killjoy":

> I see nothing fine
> when the sun shines
> I mock the poet singing praise in parliament
> I cause a predicament
> reveal poverty
> in our liberty
> I am killjoy
> I am killjoy

Furthermore, there are poets who believe that poetry should be used to heal the wounds of the past and create a better present from which the future emerges in hope. To these poets, the picture of a traumatized society is out of tune with the spirit of national reconstruction, and should be abandoned. Accordingly, they distance themselves from poets exploring misery, pain and anguish, and focus on issues capable of bringing about a balance between psychic emotion and realistic awareness as well as detached appraisal of experience. These poets echo the contemporary critical voices that favour using poetry to build social bridges of understanding and love in South Africa. As Serote notes, "for a long time the two opposites, the ideal world and the real world, are going to form the basis of a very strong articulation on the part of writers"[14], so Cronnin also argues that:

> "A relevant South African poetry should force the actual and the desirable into the same aesthetic, linguistic and subjective space," adding that political themes in post-liberation poetry have turned to grappling with the shortfall between post-apartheid aspirations and actual realities on the ground.[15]

To this end, a series of poetic perceptions of the contemporary state of the country have emerged which combine sharp evocations of the contemporary dark social reality with optimistic expressions of encouragement and hope. Rustum Kozain in "February Moon: Cape Town", for example, poeticizes the contemporary dark social reality:

> My land's an expanse of rubble
> and slogans, charters, accords.
> Handshakes commit chattering guns
> to obscenity and soap operas.
> Every day, violence kitsches itself
> onto front pages ....
> (Rustum Kozain's "February Moon: Cape town". Excerpt)

Clearly, any close analysis of how life is experienced in South Africa at present will magnify the huge discrepancies of wealth, education, and access to resources. The widespread discontent and anger issuing from this finds expression in sporadic violence that has turned free South Africa into "an expanse of rubble", as the poem posits. The disappearance of unity and cohesion occasioned by sporadic violence is responsible for the sharp social divisions and re-fragmentation of South Africa, as if to say that the ghost of apartheid was yet to be finally laid to rest. Leboyang Mashile deeply shares this vision of a fractured South Africa as demonstrated in her poem, "AB":

> ... South Africa is a fractured mirror
> A paradox of schizophrenic selves
> Who don't talk to one another
> Who fear each other
> Who revere each other
> Who loathe
> And pretend
> And try and blend
> With each other
>
> And this is the time you can become
> The greatest substance of your dreams
> Demand healing selves

The encouragement contained in the poem is meant to inspire confidence and hope among the people whose mind is yet to live out the excoriating and haunting apartheid past. In "Resurrection", the poet celebrates a new South Africa where racism will not have a place:

> And Yesterdays nightmares
> Becomes today's dreams
> Colour was a fact
> The sum of all
> Is rich
> Is scorned
> Is reborn

In "Sister", a poem in her collection of poems titled *Black Candles,* Leboyang turns to the touchy issue of gender, decrying female neglect, and advocating for genuine concern and sensitivity to issue of female empowerment in the new South Africa:

> ... *the sons of oppression*
> never gave sisters
> loaves to feed the hungry fury in their bellies

> nor did they teach them to fish for spirit
>
> So I pray
> to the voices that whisper in my soft curves
> for the lionesses of my blood
> to hear the songs of the cool reeds
> to feel the green blood beat of cataclysm on their breasts
> and to know the embrace of freedom
> in nourishing silences
> where their radiant ebony vessels
> are reflections of their souls.
>
> (Leboyang Mashile's *Black Candles*, 2008)

Leboyang's poetry reflects the belief that, unlike in the apartheid era when the "Whiteman" is the arch enemy, in the aftermath of socio-political changes in post-apartheid South Africa, the enemy isn't really clear in the way it used to be. It is an incredibly sensitive, complicated struggle with many dimensions, but the site for that struggle is inside. The poems in her collection, *A Ribbon of Rhythm* (2005), also speak about life in the new South Africa, particularly on issues like diversity and unity of the "Rainbow Nation", the status of women, violence, and vulnerability of the individual.

Despite the celebratory lyrical tone, cynicism still skirts Leboyang's poetry, a cynicism reflecting the mood of the times. Rather than the triumphal march into the future defined by nationalist discourse, time is, at worst, experienced by many South Africans as circular, as promises made never seem to be carried further and — on a national level — social betterment is painfully slow, and in the experience of some, especially the poorest and most marginalized, is non-existent. Promises about prosperity remain unrealized, while the widening gap between the rich and the poor indicates that very little has happened to secure public confidence in the new nation.

As apartheid significantly stunted the full expression of humanity among both black and white, the sensitive domain of some poets shifted from the borders of exploration of society to a concern with personal issues in ways which challenge existing societal norms and open up fresh spheres of contemplation, as can be seen Tsehlana's "I Write to ...":

> I write to untie the knots
> that lump my throat
> and turn into splitting headaches
>
> I write to wipe the tears
> as the pages of pain
> scroll from my thumbs
> smudging my mascara.
>
> I write that they may know
> I became even stronger
> when my heart was broken
> by culture, church,
> civilization
> even
> syphilization.
> I write to share with you the quiet
> revolution raging inside my brain ...
> ("I write to ...")

The Postcolonial Debate in South African Poetry

However, it is clear that the degree of subjectivity in contemporary South African literature has widened the parameters of personal expression. In some instances, there is an inclination to use literature to refurbish traditional notions of "the individual" and compartmentalize subjective experience into emotional and psychological categories divorced from the social. Liberation saw a reiteration, among more conservative and liberal poets, of the model of the discrete individual of liberal theorizing. This was combined with a notion that poetry should act as a bulwark against political, or public, demands. The Johannesburg poet, Lionel Abrahams, praises the vision of those white liberals of the past who "chose a solution that relied on gradual moral and philosophical transformation within the will of individuals." From this viewpoint, the individual poet should eschew what Cape Town poet, Stephen Watson, calls "any position of subservience to history." The poet is seen as a watchdog against "social engineering" or any invasion of politics or public discourse into personal space. In such a view, poetry, especially lyric poetry, is a means of preserving and expressing a non-reducible "inner life,"[16] and sensitizing individuals through acts of communication between writer and reader. Poetry is perceived as indirectly serving the same mooted cause as liberal politics; to "serve the well-being of one's fellow creatures" based on the grounds of one's own "artistic integrity."[17] Abrahams is a remarkably candid example of the contradictions of contemporary South African liberals' self-image: a self-abnegation, hand in hand, with a somewhat patronizing certainty in the ultimate rectitude of their ideological position. He makes clear the role each liberal follower — including each writer — bears in this:

> The more developed — that is to say the more individualized the identity, the more significant the identification. ... Solidarity on the one hand and the imaginative act of human identification on the other requires entirely different things of the self .... This difference accounts for the human and aesthetic poverty of so much political writing: it addresses itself not outwards to the unpredictable heart of the stranger who is your other self .... But there is the other side. The opening of our society lends a new urgency to the maintenance of our standards as individuals and as bearers of our inherited culture .... We have to guard our own, not against others but, in the first place, for ourselves, and, in the second place, for others, our compatriots, against the time when, if ever, they may choose to share it, for the future of the land.[18]

If there is one theme that seems to unite many poets of different persuasions at present, it is that of the individual in search of his or her putative identity. Historically, both apartheid and its opponents came to reduce the diversity of the South African population into the confines of four essential races (or "four nations"), even as apartheid, for its own purposes, both emphasized and fossilized Africans' division into separate ethnic groups. Mirroring debates in a wider South African intellectual context, expressions of identity among poets tend to vacillate wildly between those intent on stressing the hybrid nature of South Africans, and those who articulate their essential sense of belonging inside a group, however this is defined. Some poets can be seen to imbricate these potentially contradictory urges within a sense of personal identity.

At present, robust national discourses at work through the commercial and state media emphasize explorations of the self in search of a "true" identity. Yet, the topography of South African identity consciousness clearly shows that many wish to use notions of authenticity and cultural or racial knowledge. However, while some poets, like Dikobe Wa Mogale, who stress that the poetics of their art is a response to an ongoing racial divide between white and black based on privilege and access to resources, contending that 'art is a weapon of struggle"; it will be valid and sound as long as there still predominate, two contending cultures, namely the cultures of the oppressor and oppressed. Others, like Bila, insist that the black-white divide remains strong, and refute any suggestion that whites or blacks are a homogeneous group. Mzi Mahola, the most vocal of these, in his poetry gives effect to the loss of traditional and indigenous forms of knowledge and expression in rapidly modernizing nation, and the implications this holds for the future. Mahola's poetry gives space to themes surrounding growing up in a rural community in the Eastern Cape. Other poets have involved themselves in a searching for "roots" through poetry, reaching back to what they believe will be a more authentic identity based on the retrieval of value systems ravaged by colonialism. This kind of poetry tends to combine castigations of present global and local inequalities with invocations of iconic figures from the history of the colonized, in poems which vary from superficial hagiography to insightful analyses of the connection of past injustices to present inequalities.

In her "A Poem for Sarah Baartman," Diana Ferrus addresses the slave woman taken from the Cape and exhibited as a "freak" and "scientific curiosity" in Europe two hundred years ago, her essence being reason enough for her public admiration and zest. In many ways the poem's aesthetic is in the subjective mode, using symbolic and romantic depiction to create identity, seen in terms of images of origin and the legitimacy of one's possession of "the land." The last line of the poem is remarkably original in demonstrating the journey motif as an exercise in self-fashioning and self-discovery:

> I've come to take you home –
> home, remember the veld?
> The lush green grass beneath the big oak trees
> ... I have made your bed at the foot of the hill,
> your blankets are covered in buchu and mint,
> the protease stand in yellow and white
> and the water in the stream chuckles sing-songs
> as it hobbles along over little stones.
>
> I have come to wrench you away –
> away from the poking eyes
> of the man-made monster
> who lives in the dark
> with his clutches of imperialism
> who dissects your body bit by bit
>
> ... I offer my bosom to your weary soul
> I will cover your face with the palm of my hands
> I will run my lips over lines in your neck
> I will feast my eyes on the beauty of you ...
> I have come to take you home
> where I will sing for you

for you have brought me peace.
(Diana Ferrus' "A Poem for Sarah Baartman")

There are other voices that explore similar terrain, but use markedly different modes of perception and utterance. The work of Motsapi, for instance, mobilizes and employs a range of references embodying exemplary values seen to inhere in pre-colonial African kingdoms and contemporary African-American jazz to make statements about contemporary African realities. Through these means, he constructs a poetry that recreates a positive image for Africa, shatters the myth of European superiority and resists a global network of oppression. This is particularly evident in his "Drum Intervention":

> What shade / what shadow
> Takes over the land so
>
> ... I've known you so
> With receding suns & invading sands
> No calm but the ominous violin
> Of incessant flies
> Your history a knot of storms
> Reprobate seers & hip healers
> The speak / speed of your drums
> Now drowned to a croak
> By the convenient noises
> Of popular music
>
> I've known you so
> Seed left too long
> In the sun
> An eventual death
> In the refugee camps
> Cos we said no
> To the scum of politicks
> ... only de poor suffer
> Only de poor suffer.
> (Motsakpi's "Drum Intervention")

At worst, the poetry of identity formation can be said to have become pronouncedly fashionable, and this tendency does have its critics. Press observes:

> The interface between people's psychological collaboration in identities and the fact that identities are created by social means is not innate. ... I don't pretend for a moment that they don't exist in the daily texture of people's lives. But they are not the defining moments of reality for people: I think poverty, hunger, loneliness are just as strong.[19]

While Ari Sitas voices a determination to struggle against the false new ethnic sentiments being remembered and reinvented, there are poets who question any easy correlation made between race and class by giving expression to a political poetry highlighting the inequalities surrounding race under global capitalism. Rampolokeng, for one, notes that "one weakness of our past political engagements was the way apartheid made us posit everything on a racial basis — when everyone knows that the class thing was lurking there and was far more threatening".

Rampolokeng here echoes the prevailing postcolonial view that it is premature to claim that the advent of majority rule produced a cultural situation in which unified aesthetics of the past were rendered obsolete either by narratives of the racial assertion which inform colonial writing, or of the oppressed self in the writing of the oppressed, are no longer possible in stories of social actuality. Nonetheless, many contemporary poets, white and black inclusive, have sought to explore new and interstitial spaces of identity, and express experiences more hybrid than has traditionally been possible. Many critics, for instance, see the challenge for South African poets as finding ways to remove racial consciousness between them, and stop being anything else but poets. The result has been, at best, poetry of a rich complexity, as evident in Immanuel Suttner's "De tetrarch hammer" which appropriates Rastafarian discourse rhythms to comment on his white, Jewish roots:

> Um yisrael wen 'cross to babylon
> started callin his self irwin cohn
> writin for de newspaper in Washington
> bin nice n pleasant to everyone
>
> or got Hasidic in ol New York
> bow in to de hot air in de rabbi's talk
> dancing to de beet of de fals messiah stalk
> dey say he gonna come if we stay away from pork
>
> me i say me eyes is full o sand
> i gotta smash de idols bilt by de fader's hand
> like trotsky done or like avram's stand
> and bild mehself meh own promise land
>   (Immanuel Suttner's "De tetrarch hammer")

Quite a number of poets handle themes dealing with democracy and the "Rainbow Nation". Since liberation, South Africa has been configured in media and politicians' pronouncements as being a "rainbow nation": a conglomeration of different races, cultures and persuasions living in harmony and equality. In concord with this, a multiplicity of voices, interpretations and "stories" are now celebrated in literary forums. Yet, the social reality is less ideal, as can be seen in the manner in which this diversity relates to harder political questions, where the challenge facing South Africans remains how to forge some kind of national unity, share space and yet sustain plurality, diversity and debate. At the moment, such celebration is almost always linked with a promotion of political pluralism, conceived to work in much the same style as it has always functioned in the capitalist state. If taken into the realm of identity and culture, such pluralism is often idealistically portrayed, as in Mabuza's "Today You Are Not Well":

> We must also borrow
>   From the rainbow

> Such heat, such energy such cleansing water
> And judge just so much that we may
> Fuse them into finest colours
> And splash them across the sky

Yet what precisely this "rainbow" consists of, or should consist of, remains open to disagreement. Chris Mann uses *South Africans: A Set of Portrait Poems* (2006), a whole collection of poems, to explicitly embody the "rainbow nation". In majority of the poems, individuals from different origins and backgrounds are depicted against the social backdrop of the country around the time of the first elections. Thus, the book provides portraits of people as individuals, and in groups of individuals, giving a glimpse of the astonishing diversity of the people who are South Africans. The work's plural aesthetics is strongly balanced against a severe test of the individual subjects of poems on pro-liberal values. For Mann:

> Business and political leaders in the new South Africa are living in an intellectual climate not unlike that of the Renaissance. The Medicis were part of a rising business class that cast aside the despotism of the medieval church and rediscovered their potential as humans. Many new South Africans, both black and white, are thrusting aside the despotism of apartheid, tribalism and Marxism and finding fresh creative energies.[20]

While intellectuals honour the emergence of hybrid subjectivity, the advertising of South Africa as a "rainbow nation" with its overtones of mutual acceptance and accommodation gives a falsely optimistic picture of triumph against social divisions on the ground, in a scenario where disparities of wealth and competition over limited resources can become, literally, 'deathly'. This indeed inspires Horwitz's remarks that as far as the rainbow nation is concerned, "in the absence of broader political direction, the attempt by the media to literally create the new culture is a disaster because it's superficial."[21] Often, a facile pluralism is assumed, where the individuals who emerge from different languages and cultures are regarded as now meeting on an equal footing, with scant regard for present inequalities. The individual is farcically placed within a "race" or "culture"; and literature is assumed to act out an embodiment, in diverse forms, of communication between individuals thus placed. This is in sharp contrast to poets like Rampolokeng or Motsapi, whose works illustrate how the "human" is a space intersected by material constraints and subject to the manipulations of the powerful. According to Rampolokeng, in his "The New Vampires", free South Africa makes:

> Humanity a stool
> between parted buttocks of international conspiracy
> death is the coldest currency
> ... it foreign exchanges in the silence of finance's terms
> dictates of the new vampires
> (Lesego Rampolokeng's "The New Vampires", excerpt)

Thus, while it is apposite to say that current struggles in South Africa are "emblematic of broader human issues," the poem's proviso is that people live in a world dominated by capitalism which is far from solving the universal human problems. At the moment, the individual's ability to find fulfillment is curtailed by social and economic forces outside his or her control, and often globally distant. As Roshila Nair notes in "Fanon's Land":

> Love still finds me here
> In the post-colonial hour,
> Here
> Among the politics of viruses
> And neo-liberal economic policies,
> Here among the grand things
> That have curled around us
> And sprouted wings
> Like god's heavenly creatures
> Vainly trying to transport us to paradise
> Here in Fanon's no-man's land

> We are beginning to learn
> How to make everything
> Out of nothing again.
> (Roshila Nair's "Fanon's Land")

Whatever the case, poets are crawling out of every corner of South Africa, from jazz joints, college campuses, art galleries and quaint restaurants, and urban landscapes, holding phallic pens to challenge uncritical acceptance of foreign cultures, particularly American, generally equated by youths as a post-colonial subjugation mode. Thus there seem to be a blend between the poetry of socio-political and economic agitation, and the personal type in which poets responded to topical issues of the day from personal angles, while some poets still hold fast to the possibility that they speak for a wider community.

Beginning from Mashile, however, there are divergent conceptions of what sustenance of struggle in the present South African context means, even though everybody agrees that all poets need to mediate in all crises-prone situations. An iconic figure for a younger generation of urban, self-assertive, upwardly-mobile black women, Mashile constantly voices a poetry that demands gender and racial equality, awareness and empowerment, as in "Sisters":

> I see the wisdom of eternities
> In ample thighs
> Belying their presence as adornments
> To the temples of my sisters
> Old souls breathe
> In the comfort of chocolate thickness
> That suffocates Africa's angels
> Who dance to the rhythm
> Of the universe's womb
> Though they cannot feel
>
> Its origins in their veins
> ... I pray to the voices
> That whisper in my soft curves

For the lionesses of my blood
To hear the songs of the cool reeds

There are indications here that the creation of a better-educated urban woman is an issue that needs to be resolved to take a new South Africa to the next level; to strive for a new national identity and to establish and authenticate a new, self-knowingly hybrid version of that identity. At the same time, it is clear that certain forms of identity are regarded as more authentic than others, with African values serving as models for change. Thus Kgafela Magogodi, in his poem "Bohemia," excoriates the kind of person who:

Somersaults
In its mother's womb
Pops out feet first
No labour pains
... It skips the nappy
For a pair of jeans
It suckles
From a pint of beer
... It is zimzim come to jozi
... It is chasing fame
In rocky street
It is not foolish
Just learnt
To speak pure English
Thru blocked nose

Nevertheless, there are those who continue to express themselves critically and openly about the social ills of South Africa, and the complacency among some of the youth. This can be seen not only on the printed page but among some of those who span the gap between poetry and hip-hop culture and music. Marlon Burgess' poetry provides an incisive commentary on socio-political issues, consumer culture, and the emergent political leadership:

We were in bondage

> Now we are worse than we ever were.
> We keep ourselves afloat on a very thin dream
> Celebrating ten years of de"mock"racy
> And we thought our liberation was from racism?
> We're all in a cell we can't see
> As Isidingo snatches at Generations of those who Owned the Mines
> Wah wah revolution
> Wah wah revolution
> It must be kak confusing
> From being abused to doing the abusing.

Poetry can be a powerful tool for modeling and shaping individual subjectivity, and hence social behaviour. The crucial question, consequently, is the relation of this desired subjectivity to social issues in any society. In new South Africa, poetry may help highlight the "model citizen" required by the State in its current phase of transition and change.

The issue here could be put more starkly: poetry is being imbued with demands which are simply new versions of the "solidarity literature" regarded as outdated after liberation, albeit in a less obvious form. As Sandile Ngidi notes in his poem "But Nations Love Their Poets":

> Freedom has come my friend
> You are now truly free
> To write and sing as your heart pleases
> Now pursue art for art's sake
>
> ... It's that age for your rage to be tamed
> Your tongue can do with some English manners
> We no longer need your song friend
> Your slogans have no place in freedom square
> ... Discard nostalgic fantasies about beloved Africa
> Now the future is oily bright and as shiny as gold
> ... No! my friend, no shouting now
> For God's sake be reasonable now
> No! you can't jump the queue
> Send me a proposal first
> But my hands are tied ....

Conclusion

Reading contemporary South African poetry, one is left with a vertiginous sense of the contradictions of a country which is constructing itself out of heterogeneous fragments and fortuitous juxtapositions of images, memories, citations, and allusions drawn from its splintered histories. The problem, of course, is that the ideological and expressive baggage residing in these "splintered histories" does not seem to want to go away. In South Africa, poetry has become illustrative of disagreement over political, social, and psychological issues, as well as aesthetic and evaluative criteria. A potent ideological function still resides in the country's poetry after liberation; and the ceaseless reiteration of "rainbow nation" clichés and celebrations of expressive freedom by critics mask the fact that there are powerful forces at work seeking to utilize the medium for a new hegemony in favour of the present ruling classes and their sanitized versions of individual subjectivity and cultural, as well as national, identity. It is possible to see contemporary events in poetry in optimistic terms, but the pessimistic note expressed by Rampolokeng and some others, that the country is still doing a monkey dance for colonialism, can hardly be parried off. It is only fitting that I end this discourse with Horwitz's suggestion that in South Africa:

> Poetry won't ever die but at the moment we don't live in a time when there's clarity, when there is a clear direction. It's a time of individualism ... the sense of solidarity has broken down completely. There always were opportunists, but now it's very open and unashamed. ... No doubt our arts will reflect that...[22]

Primary Texts

Gardiner, Michael, ed. *Throbbing Ink*. Elim: Timbila, 2003.
Kozain, Rustum. *This Carting Life*. Cape Town: Kwela, 2005.
Mabuza, Lindiwe. *Voices That Lead*. Florida Hills: Vivlia, 1998.

Kgafela oa Magogodi. *Thy Condom Come*. Amsterdam: New Leaf, Mashile, Lebogang. *In a Ribbon of Rhythm*. Johannesburg: Oshun, 2005.

Metelerkamp, Joan. *Floating Islands*. Knysna: Rustica, 2001.

Mokhosi, Rose, ed. *Basadzi Voices*. Pietermaritzburg: UKZN Press, 2006.

Motsapi, Seitlhamo. *Earth Stepper / The Ocean is Very Shallow*. Grahamstown: Deep South, 1995.

New Coin 30.2 (1994).

New Coin 37.2 (2001).

Parenzee, Donald, et al. *No Free Sleeping*. Johannesburg: Botsotso, 1998.

Press, Karen. *Home*. Manchester: Carcanet, 2000.

Rampolokeng, Lesego. *Talking Rain*. Johannesburg: COSAW, 1993.

—. *The Bavino Sermons*. Durban: Gecko, 1999.

—. *The Second Chapter*. Berlin: Pantolea, 2003.

Rasebotsa, Nobantu, Meg Samuelson and Kylie Thomas, eds. *Nobody Ever Said AIDS*. Cape Town: Kwela, 2004.

Serote, Mongane. *Freedom, Lament and Song*. Cape Town: David Philip, 1997.

Siphiwe ka Ngwenya. *Soul fire Experience*. Johannesburg: Botsotso, 2005.

Suttner, Immanuel. *Hidden and Revealed*. Cape Town: Snail press, 2007.

Timbila. 5, 2005.

Tromp, Ian. *Setting Out*. Johannesburg: Snail Press, 1994.

Notes and References

1. Albert S. Gerard, *Four African Literatures* (Amheric: University of California Press, Benkeley, 1971) p. 24.
2. Gerard, p. 237.
3. Chinua Achebe, *Morning Yet on Creation Day* (London: Heinemann, 1978) p. 44.
4. Richard Wren, *African Drama Today* (London: Heinemann, 1968) p. 5.
5. Ime Ikiddeh, "Poetry and National Liberation: The Example of Agostinho Neto". *Journal of Commonwealth Literature,* October, 1986. p. 45.
6. Romanus Egudu, *Poetry and the African Predicament* (Enugu: Fourth Dimension Publishers, 1986) p. 75.
7. Egudu, 76.
8. S. Raditholo, "Tran-Colonial Poetry of South Africa." *Journal of Literature and Language Teaching*, 2001, University of Cape Town, South Africa, p. 42.
9. Raditholo, 43.
10. Robert Berold, "Interview: Lesego Rampolokeng & Ike Mboneni Muila" in Berold, *South African Poets* 138; Heather Robertson, "Talented Kgositsile Back from Obscurity," *South* 4-10 Oct. 1990.
11. Berold, 8.
12. Vonani Bila, "The Irrelevance of Prizes to Poetry," *New Coin* 41.2 (2005): 8. It could be argued that this relates to the prevalence of a wider official discourse and "multi-theoried rhetoric" which (in poet Mark Espin's words) "suggests radical argument, but which ultimately evades the dilemmas which confront us"; see Espin, "Ubuntu Bourgeoisie is Bogus," *Mail & Guardian* 9-15 May 1997.
13. Lesego Rampolokeng, "Interview," *The h.a.l.f. ranthology,* Ambush-street Corner Mixes, Mehlo-Maya, 2002 *Africa* 292 (2007) <. Thanks to Lee-Ann Pilleggi for drawing this poet to my attention.
14. Sorote qtd. in Robert Berold, "Interview: Denis Hirson,"

South African Poets on Poetry, ed. Robert Berold (Pietermaritzburg, Gecko, 2003) 79.
15. Jeremy Cronin, "The Oral and Contemporary South African Poetry," New Spaces in South African Poetry Conference, Poetry International, Rotterdam, Oct. 1998,
16. Andries Oliphant, "Inside Out: Spatial Retracing in Some Recent South African Poetry," *Sulfur* 44 (1999): 225-26.
17. Trevor James *English Literatures from the Third World* (New York: Heinemann,1986) p. 64.
18. Lionel Abrahams, *The Democratic Chorus and Individual Choice* (Johannesburg: SAIRR, 1996) 11.
19. Qtd. in Joanna Hensley and Roy Blumenthal, ed., *Of Money, Mandarins and Peasants* (Johannesburg: Homeless Talk, 2000) 89.
20. Chris Mann, "Without Patrons, Malls Will Be Our Monuments," *Business Day* 6 Jan. 1995.
21. Qtd. in Joanna Hensley and Roy Blumenthal, ed., *Of Money, Mandarins and Peasants* (Johannesburg: Homeless Talk, 2000) 89.
22. Qtd. In Hensley, p. 90.

Conclusion

I don't think that I have settled even the most basic issues in the study of modern African poetry in this study. What I have tried to do is to systematize our knowledge of a few of the main arguments which border on how modern African poetic tradition is a carrier of aesthetic, ideological and social properties undergirded by Africa's colonial and postcolonial inheritance. It is therefore the interplay of these elements that provides that tradition its distinct structure, character and essence. However, while there are other significant areas of enquiry which deserve close analytic scrutiny, an engaging discourse on modern African Poetry, for me, remains centred on the issues of art, ideology and social commitment.

As an aesthetic medium, modern African poetry is predicated on the complicated nuances of the African experience. These nuances, in their conflictual relationships, inter-connections and problematic affinities, provide the nexus between material reality as a predictable social quantity and poetry as a reflective aesthetic category. And these nuances are nothing but the historicization of the effects of ideological consciousness, no matter how defined or interpreted, on social processes which shape the African world. Without this problematic dialectic, African poetry will lose its vitality, its cogency, its social relevance, and its role as a means of communicating shared experiences.

What future has modern African poetry, one may ask, in this time and age? There is, of course, no doubt that poetic creations will remain a veritable part of African private and public life, from the rhyme-making by pre-scholars to the tentative gestures of university undergraduates whose codified poetic experiments is a form of aestheticization of learning and cultural adaptation; and from the outpourings of members of bohemian poetry clubs to the assured cadences of the tested masters. There is little doubt too that no environment, no matter how misshapen or distorted it may be and Africa is presently misshapen and distorted under the intense pressure of late, postmodern capitalism and the dematerialization of the ontology of postcoloniality by a shamanist poststructuralist discursive mode of critical intervention, will fall to produce great works of art, meaning that poetic creations still manage to get on in the midst of present-day African political economic, social and cultural drift.

The picture is not a pretty one. Mismanagement of national resources, political instability, social strife and monumental corruption by the bulk of African political leadership have combined to create a quantum flight of African cultural intelligentsia to America, Western Europe and elsewhere. The flight of these cultural elite has produced an exile or refugee community abroad. Our poets, young and old, have joined the exodus, and are presently haunting American and English universities' African Studies centres as writers-in-residence.

Our creative writers, and most especially African poets, are now an endangered species. Annihilated at home by poverty, scarcity of books and other materials and the insensitivity of African anti-intellectual rulership; and deracinated overseas where they now exist as cultural hybrids, the most unfortunate example of a symbiotic identity, they have very little to write about. They can't write well about home, for their links to their roots have been virtually severed, neither can they effectively communicate non-African experiences for the obvious fact that these are alien to them. As it stands today, no continental or international forum on the African literary process can take place in Africa for the simple reason that almost all those to be invited have deserted the continent. African poetry can no longer afford to be poetry of protest and anguish. It must become reconstructive, not as a marginal cultural force in the course of African social transformation, but as a dominant element in the task of social engineering and continental renewal. But to be ably placed to assist in these goals, Africa must be free of its numerous untutored tyrants who have virtually turned almost the whole continent into a veritable modern wasteland. It is only when this singular task is accomplished – that of democratizing and humanizing the continent – that our poetic heritage, and the living creative energy it embodies, can begin to fulfil its social obligations to society.

Bibliography

Ahmad, Aijaz. *In Theory: Classes, Nations, Literatures.* London: Verso, 1992.

Anozie, Sunday. Christopher Okigbo: *Creative Rhetoric.* London Evans, 1972.

Anyidoho, Kofi et al (eds). *Beyond Survival: African Literature and the Search for New Life.* Trenton, N.J: Africa World Press, 1999.

Ashcroft, Bill et al. *The Empire Writes Back: Theory and Practice in Postcolonial Literatures.* London and New York: Routledge, 1989.

Azikiwe Nnamdi. *Meditations.* Nsukka. African Book Company, 1977.

Bahbah, Homi. *The Location of Culture.* London: Routledge, 1994.

Bakalov, Georgi. *Selected Works.* Vol. 2. Sofia: Pisatel Press, 1963.

Boguslavsky, B.M. et al. *ABC of Dialectical and Historical Materialism.* Moscow: Progress Publishers, 1975.

Ceasaire, Aime. *Return to my Native Land.* London: Penguin Books, 1969.

Chinweizu et al. *Toward the Decolonization of African Literature.* Enugu: Fourth Dimension, 1980.

Dathorne, O.R. *African Literature in the 20th Century.* London: Heinemann, 1975.

Eagleton, Terry. *Literary Theory: An Introduction.* Oxford: Blackwell Publishing, 1983, 1996, 2008.

Egudu, Romanus. *Four Modern West African Poets.* New York: Nok Publishers, 1977.

Falola, T. et al. *Migration and Creative Expression in Africa and the African Diaspora.* North Carolina: Carolina Academic Press, 2008.

Fanon, Frantz. *The Wretched of the Earth.* Harmondsworth: Penguin Publishers, 1962.

Foucault, Michel. *New Domains.* London: Routledge, 1993

Gibbs, James and Bernth Lindfors. *Research on Wole Soyinka.* Trenton, N.J: Africa World Press, 1993.

Gugelberger, G.M. *Marxism and African Literature.* London: James Currey, Ltd, 1985.

Heron, G. *The Poetry of Okot. P' Bitek.* London: Heinemann, 1980.

Heywood, Chris ed. *Aspects of South African Literature* London: Heinemann, 1976.

Horn, Peter. *Writing my Reading: Essays on Literary Politics in South Africa.* Amsterdam: Rodopi, 1994.

Howe, Stephen. *Afrocentricism: Mythical Pasts and Imagined Homes.* London: Verso, 1999.

Jameson, Fredric. *Marxism and Form: 20th Century Dialectical Theories of Literature.* Princeton: Princeton University Press, 1974.

Jones, Eldred. *The Writing of Wole Soyinka.* 3rd Edition. London: James Curry, 1988.

Killam, Douglas. *Literature of Africa.* Westport Connecticut: Greenwood Press, 2004.

Loomba, Ania. *Colonialism/Postcolonialism.* London: Routledge, 1998.

Maduakor, Obi. *Wole Soyinka: An Introduction to His Writing.* New York: Garland Press, 1986.

Markov, Dmitry. *Socialist Literatures: Problems of Development,*

Moscow: Progress Publishers, 1984.

Minh-ha, Trinh T. *Woman, Native Order: Writing Postcoloniality and Feminism*. Bloomington: Indiana Univ. Press, 1989.

Ohaeto, Ezenwa. *Nigerian Poetry and the Poetics of Orality*. Bayreuth: Bayreuth African Studies Series, 1998.

Ojaide, Tanure. *The Poetry of Wole Soyinka*. Lagos: Malthouse, 1994.

Osofisan, Femi. *The City as Muse: Ibadan and the Efflorescence of Nigerian Literature*. Ibadan: Hope Publications Ltd, 2007.

Otiono, Nduka and Odoh Diego Okenyedo (ed). *Comouflage: Best of Contemporary Writing From Nigeria*. Yenagoa: Treasure, 2006.

Ovcharenko, A. *Socialist Realist and the Modern Literary Process*. Moscow: Novosti Press, 1978.

Parekh, Pushpa and Siga Fatima Jagne, eds. *Postcolonial African Writers: A Bio-Bibliographical Critical Sourcebook*. Westport, Connecticut: Greenwood Press, 1998

Prawer, S.S. *Karl Marx and World Literature*. Oxford: Oxford University Press. 1976.

Ramazani, Jahan. *The Hybrid Muse: Postcolonial Poetry in English*. Chicago: Univ. of Chicago Press, 2001.

Roscoe, Adrian. *Uhuru's Fire: African Literature East to South*: Cambridge: Cambridge University Press, 1977.

Rutherford, Anna. Ed. *From Commonwealth to Postcolonial*. Sydney: Dangoro Press, 1990.

Said, Edward. *Representations of the Intellectual*, London: Vintage, 1994.

_____ *Orientalism*. London: Routledge and Kegan Paul, 1978.

Sanders, Mark. *Complicities: The Intellectual and Apartheid*. USA: Duke University Press, 2002.

Tiffin, Chris and Alan Lawson, eds. *De-scribing Empire:*

Postcolonialism and Textuality. London: Routledge, 1994.
Tolstoy, Leo. *Resurrection.* Harmondsworth Penguin, 1966
Vasov, Ivan. *Collected Works. Vol. I.* Sofia: Bulgarsky Pisatel Publishers, 1957.
Wa Thiong'o, Ngugi. *Homecoming.* London: Heinemann, 1972.
_____ *Writers in Politics.* London: Heinemann, 1980.
_____ *Moving the Centre. Struggle for Cultural Freedoms.* London: Heinemann, 1993.
Williams, Patrick and Laura Chrisman, eds. *Colonial Discourse and Postcolonial Theory: A Reader.* New York: Columbia Univ Press, 1994.
Wright, Derek. *Wole Soyinka Revisited.* New York: Twayne, 1993.
Young, R. *Colonial Desire: Hybridity in Theory, Culture and Race.* London: Routledge, 1995.

www.ingramcontent.com/pod-product-compliance
Lightning Source LLC
Chambersburg PA
CBHW010832230426
43668CB00019BA/2414